I0408266

SASQUATCH ENCOUNTERS

True Tales Of Bigfoot

GARY AND WENDY SWANSON

Copyright © 2017 Wendy and Gary Swanson
All rights reserved.

Published by Swanson Literary Group
ISBN: 1542500311
ISBN-13: 978-1542500319

Other books by the authors:

They Saw Sasquatch
Bigfoot Uncovered
Tracking Sasquatch
Sasquatch! Reports From the Field
Bigfoot Adventures
On the Trail of Sasquatch
Sasquatch is Out There
Squatchin': Study Guide and Field Handbook for Tracking Sasquatch
Hiking Sasquatch Country: Best Hikes In Southern Oregon

Skinwalkers Shapeshifters and Native American Curses
The Last Skinwalker
We Survived Native American Witches, Curses & Skinwalkers
Skinwalker: Guardian of the Last Portal

GARY AND WENDY SWANSON

CONTENTS

INTRODUCTION

Probably the most often asked question by readers is," I do a lot of hiking, and if there are Sasquatch out there, why have I never seen one?" The answer by those in the know is, "Have you ever seen a cougar? A fox? A wolf?" The list could go on and on, but the best answer is that "Human beings are noisy!"

We do not have bare, padded feet. We have noisy clothing, shoes, keys and change in our pockets, etc. No matter how silent we think we are being, nothing can possibly compare with an animal's stealth. They have fur, padded and silent feet, they can hear twenty times better than humans. They can feel the slightest footfall; they can smell human beings from miles away. When you compare mans' ability to an animal's for stealthy passage in our outdoors is like comparing the patter of a light mist to a hailstorm on a tin roof.

Before moving to Southern Oregon, we had traveled across the United States and met people who claimed to have either seen or had encountered Sasquatch, but we never entered into any serious studies. It wasn't until we found ourselves living among so many people who are avid believers; we began to see that the majority people who have had a sighting or experienced an encounter with these creatures are quite reticent and seldom volunteer more than bits and pieces of their contact. Once you have experienced a sighting or an encounter firsthand, you end up with a mixed bag of emotions. On one hand you want to jump up on a soapbox and tell the world, but on the other hand, like most of us who truly love the outdoors and the solitude that one can experience in the remote places, you come away with a protective feeling that makes one hesitant when it comes to disclosure of an event that could bring droves of speculators tramping through our precious seclusion.

Call it selfish, perhaps it is, but humankind has a history of overreacting and causing devastation to our most important national treasures, so it makes one cautious about sharing such potentially calamitous discoveries. For these reasons we found a need to tread lightly, and although we have identified areas where sightings and encounters have occurred, once you experience the ruggedness of our more remote mountain regions, you soon come to understand that a ten foot difference in a trail or point of interest can make a difference of miles as to where it ultimately ends.

Those who believe in the existence of Sasquatch come from all walks of life, including some very educated individuals. For example, the Associated Press reported on September 5, 2012 in an article entitled "Academia is a lonely place for Sasquatch hunter Jeff Meldrum." Dr. Don Jeffrey (Jeff) Meldrum is a full professor of anatomy and anthropology at Idaho State University and the A.P. article refers to Dr. Meldrum's book "Sasquatch: Legend Meets Science," from which they state the following, "In the realm of field work; Meldrum is certain Sasquatch lives." They quote Dr. Meldrum as saying, "He's a solitary creature with a lifespan of at least 20 years, rarely reproduces and finds remote places to curl up and die." Dr. Meldrum further states that, "Having studied the molds of footprints 16 inches or bigger, indicate creatures more than seven feet tall and weighing 700 pounds." The A.P. article continues with, "Sasquatch is not the biblical Cain as some members of the Church of Jesus Christ of Latter-day Saints believe. Meldrum, who is Mormon, said no evidence supports the notion." Dr. Meldrum's office is filled with over 200 molds of Sasquatch footprints. He also has hair samples from animals such as deer, bear, elk, and then the unknown samples; which remain unidentified and are suspected Sasquatch samples.

We have been very careful to protect our contributors' identities, and even where the individuals have given us permission to disclose their information, when we realized how many of these experiences were seemingly indisputable as to their validity, we chose to protect everyone who shared their encounters with us.

Several of our contributors said they were relieved to be able to tell their stories, as it makes it difficult to have had such an experience that they couldn't share, even in many cases with their closest friends. This way, they will be among friends in this book.

We have tried to make very few changes except to assist in some spelling corrections where necessary and slight changes to clarify our writer's meanings while maintaining the integrity of their own words. These stories are unedited for content.

While it is true that the majority of Sasquatch sightings have happened in the Pacific Northwest; due to the friends we have made from our books *They Saw Sasquatch* and *Hiking Sasquatch Country* we have received submissions from other parts of the country. When we began collecting data on Bigfoot sightings from our Northwest home, we had no idea that Sasquatch have been seen over most of the United States, and we thank all of our contributors for sharing their experiences and the very fascinating stories of their family members.

Many of these stories came in after our cutoff date for inclusion in our book, "They Saw Sasquatch," and as the encounters kept coming, we decided to print this sequel.

The sighting by Evel Knievel's father was told by Nic Knievel who was a personal friend of mine (Gary Swanson). Al Capone's shooting incident was found in a very old article that was prepared for submission to the Chicago Sun Times, but for reasons unknown was never sent in; possibly due to fear, as "Big Al" still had influence, even from Alcatraz! There are several stories that came from the descendants of gold miners which did not surprise us. Gold mining is a lonely job even today, and many of these men kept journals as they spent so much time without the company of another human being.

Unless otherwise attributed, the photos accompanying these events are from the author's collection in their book "Hiking Sasquatch Country" and from their extensive photo catalog.

We, as the publishers, do not guarantee the accuracy of the stories submitted, and we can only share these encounters and let our readers make their own determination as to their validity.

This is how we first heard it!

Welcome to Bigfoot country!

Gary Swanson and Wendy Swanson

If you have had a personal encounter or sighting of a Sasquatch that you would like to see published in our next book, please send the details and any accompanying photos to:

swanliterary@gmail.com

If your story is published you will receive a copy of the book as our thanks.

AL CAPONE SHOOTS SASQUATCH

It seems strange to me that way back when I had never even heard of such thing as a Sasquatch, it appears that there may have really been, but maybe without the instant news coverage and communication such as it is today, nobody made a big deal of it?

My uncle, James Whelpley, left a pretty detailed account of his life in records that my aunt discovered after his passing. Uncle Jim was an early professional boxer who fought under the name of Jimmy Walker until a heart problem cut short his career. Supposedly, his was the first televised heart operation. After his recovery, he became a Chicago taxi cab driver and I remember sitting spellbound as a child while Uncle Jim told stories of life in the Windy City while my parents and grandparents were gathered around.

The Whelpleys lived very near the site of the St. Valentine's Day Massacre, and I remember my aunt and uncle telling about hearing the gunfire, and Uncle Jim seemed to know right away what had happened, while my aunt said she was not aware until the news became public.

After Uncle Jim's death, his personal diary revealed that he was more than just aware of the Capone organization; he had some close association. A story of one of his trips with some of the big boss's people showed that he knew and had met Al Capone himself; and Jim had been a guest of a close friend who was one of the boss's main people.

Jim and I were close and I welcomed his annual visits to see my grandparents and parents in Minnesota. He even taught me how to drive a car. Jimmy never talked about his mob connections, and had I known about it, I would have pestered him with nonstop questions. After reading the side notes in his diary, I understand his secrecy!

One story he had written out almost seemed like he had intended to submit it to a magazine, as it was addressed "Dear Sirs," but no further heading had been filled in. Aunt Ruth told me he mentioned to her something about sending a story to the Chicago Sun Times, but never did. She said he had prepared it because the editor wanted to print it.

The following is the story he had prepared to submit:

> I became friends with many of Al Capone's people, as they owned a bar near where I lived and they even told me to stay home on the upcoming St. Valentine's Day. When I asked why, they just answered, "Stay inside and you'll know later." I was never in on any of their activities, but I was usually asked to keep my taxicab available for quick trips. My dispatcher was okay with my sort of being "on call," as he was also a frequent visitor at their bar; besides, the tips were out of this world! These men often chartered my cab for trips, as they were always under observation and their license plates were on file. Nobody could get information on who was in a cab if dispatch wouldn't talk.
>
> One day my friend Nick said his boss wanted to charter my cab for a trip to Wisconsin, so my dispatcher set it up and off I went with Nick and two of his associates. I

found out on the way there that Mr. Capone owned a huge property in northern Wisconsin that was like 400 acres in size.

We finally arrived at the property near Couderay, Wisconsin and it was really wild and beautiful with trees, hills and just great scenery. We pulled into the drive, and after Nick was recognized by the man at the gate, he moved a car that blocked the entrance and we drove up the hill to an impressive two-story stone house to what must have been at least an eight car garage, and I drove into an empty stall. Nick pointed out covered slots in the walls that he said were gun ports. There were two circular guard towers made of stone probably 15 or 20 feet high. There was a separate caretaker's residence where we were shown to rooms.

The place was beautiful and nothing like I imagined could even exist in the 1920's. The main house was astounding, with a monstrous fireplace also made of stone. I think the walls must have been over a foot thick and all stone and cement.

I gathered that our trip was to prepare the place for Al Capone's visit since the snow and ice were now gone from the lake, and deliveries were being made of supplies and service people were all over doing lawns and cleanup down at the private lake that Nick said was about 40 acres in size. I walked around with Nick and the other two just observing while Nick carried out a list of instructions he had on a clipboard.

Once when Nick and I went down to the lake, I asked

him why there was a gated road going down to the large dock, because the main gate way up at the road should have been good enough to stop a tank. Nick explained, on instructions that my life was on the line if I ever spoke of it (which until writing this down since Mr. Capone is out of the picture now, so I feel safe to do so); this place was not all for the boss's relaxation; it was purchased for its location. He went on to say the lake, during the long summer, received a steady traffic of seaplanes bringing bootlegged whiskey from Canada. Nick allowed me to ask enough questions so I could fathom the enormity of this huge operation.

What little local law there was in this remote location was on the Capone payroll, so a steady flow of booze landed, unloaded and went direct to Chicago and Milwaukie by a steady convoy of trucks. There were moving trucks, mattress trucks, furniture trucks and every description of haulers imaginable; and the planes even landed at night with a system of kerosene road flares on floating platforms to light up the lake.

I didn't get to see the landings because we were there to open the operation for the summer, and crews were cutting and clearing out the shallow growing weeds and bulrushes, and the first shipments were due to start the following week..

I remember that we made a trip to Hayward, Wisconsin to stock up on supplies for our group that consisted of cigars, some wine, and snack items like peanuts, popcorn and chips. On another side trip we stopped at a bar where I was introduced to the owner, a man named

Ralph, who Nick mentioned after we left, was Al Capone's brother. Nick said that Ralph wasn't involved with Al's business, but I wish I had known who he was beforehand; of course I figured that Nick had not told me because he knew I might ask the wrong question. I tried not to ask too many questions, and Nick and I had an understanding that I would never speak about anything that I saw.

One evening, as several of us were sitting around the huge fireplace in the main house, a man whom I only knew as "Whit" began relating a strange story of Al Capone shooting at what he said was an "Ape-man." Whit explained that Mr. Capone had been visiting at the Little Bohemia Lodge over on Little Star Lake near Manitowish Lake on Highway 51, and the owners, Emily and Hank Voss, who these men all seemed to know, told Mr. Capone of having trouble with a big creature they said resembled a huge ape.

They told Al that they had checked with the authorities and there were no reports of any circus or zoo having lost any of their large beasts, but Emily and Hank said the creature kept breaking into their outbuildings, killing chickens and stealing food; fruits and vegetables kept disappearing from their root cellar.

Well, Whit said that since Mr. Capone and several of "the boys" were staying at Little Bohemia for a few days; Al said he'd take a stroll along the lakeshore along toward dusk. Whit continued, saying that after dinner that evening, Mr. Capone went for his usual stroll, smoking his cigar, while Whit and three others followed at a respectful distance, as "the boss" liked to walk off his dinner and relax with a smoke. He called this, "His private time," as this was as close as he could allow himself to be alone.

Little Bohemia Lodge ~ Image by the Federal Bureau of Investigation

Suddenly Whit said, "The boss reached into his coat, withdrawing his Colt .32 auto and began rapidly firing it at the trees along Little Star Lake." He went on to say that when they got up to where Al was, he pointed the empty pistol at the trees and said, "There's a damned ape out there get the &#%!@?! shotguns!" Whit said there they were in their suits charging through the brush at the shoreline in knee deep water and bulrushes and cattails and all they found were a couple of muddy holes where something had run just ahead of them, because the holes were filling with water as they got there. It was getting dark by then and whatever it was must have by then got into the forest, so they were forced to turn back. They went back to Shy Town the next day, but the locals at the lodge told them on their next trip up that they had several more "ape" sightings over the year.

Well, after Whit finished his story, several of the others chimed in with stories that they had heard from people in the area that these occurrences had happened also around the town of Tomahawk, Wisconsin.

I found myself believing in the creature, as nobody questioned Al Capone!

I am submitting this after reading the story in your paper about the ape-like creature that was reported by those campers in the Sheboygan area. Your article asked if any other people had seen such an animal.

James Whelpley

****

Being as how Uncle Jim never got to publish his story, perhaps it would be of interest to the readers of your Sasquatch book you advertised on the "Sasquatch Watch" page on the Internet.

Donny Burrow ~ Duluth, Minnesota

MINERS AND BIGFOOT

I have been a gold miner for most of my 57 years. The mining laws in Oregon have followed California, and the BLM seems like they keep looking for every possible reason to close access roads into our public lands. The excuses they use to keep citizens out of the mountains and push out the hard working miners range from protecting fish populations to fear of contaminating forests, and danger of forest fires.

Most of us gold miners find it necessary to also work other jobs as well as mining since it has been so up and down. My mining experience has been confined to the areas around the Rogue River and within the mountains in close proximity to the old Gold Bug mine area in the Mt. Rueben district. This area has a long history of mining and activity was up and down as gold values slowly decreased.

I was part of the partnership with the PYX mine and several others. When one of our partners forgot to maintain the generator and it burned up, rather than spend $10,000 on a new one, we just kind of walked away, and I saw when you (meaning Gary Swanson) filed the claim and then you gave it to the Josephine County Historical Society for a fundraising raffle. I bought a bunch of raffle tickets and a friend of mine got the winning ticket. He said the charge holes I had drilled years ago were still ready to be blasted and the mine was just as we had left it, except for the fact that we had scrapped the generator and the mine car tracks had been removed and sold for scrap.

Pyx Mine Entrance ~ The mine was donated and raffled to raise money for the Josephine County Historical Society

Bill said the upper tunnel was never reopened, but after he won it, he bought a small travel trailer that he brought down to that ridge above the mine adit, and brought his wife and kids along for a while and camped out so he could work longer hours. I saw him not long ago at the Armadillo

Mining Shop in Grants Pass and he said he only kept the PYX for six months before he sold it for a ton of money! He said he got something over $20,000 for it and made money while he worked it, and the raffle tickets only cost him a couple hundred dollars!

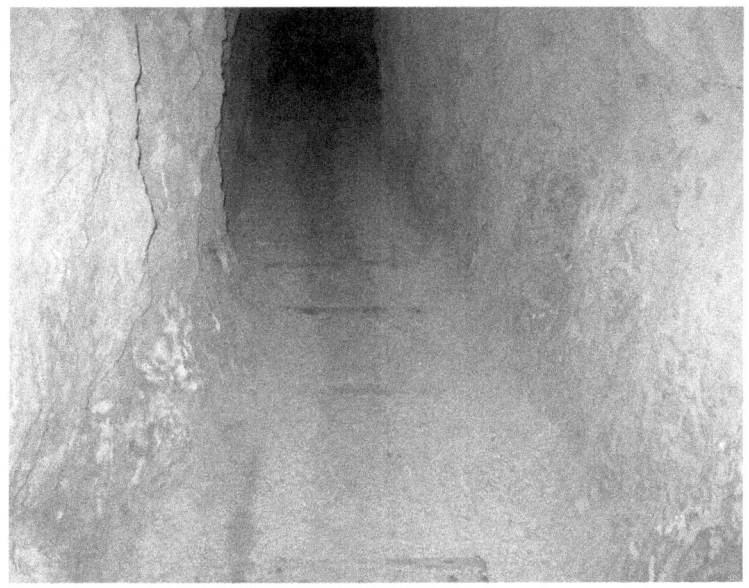

Inside the PYX Mine

I asked him if he had done well and he said he was making good profits for a one-man operation, but some creature was scaring hell out of his family. His wife and kids said a big bear-like animal had pushed a pine tree over from the hill above and it landed on the roof of the trailer. His wife had run outside when it landed, and the kids were yelling and pointing up the hill over the second shaft where she saw a large brown animal climbing up on the ridge. She said it climbed by using its front paws to pull itself up by grabbing tree trunks; and she said it was not a bear! Their kids thought it was a "wookiee" from the Star Wars movie only it was a darker brown.

Bill had to drop everything to take his family back home, and when he got back, he said the door had been torn off the trailer and it had been trashed inside. Something had torn everything apart and there were long brown hairs stuck in the screen door. He found muddy footprints of huge bare feet on the floor and food packages were ripped open and things were torn and shredded! Right after that he sold the mine to a guy from back east and he packed up and left.

This brings me to why I'm writing to you now. As I mentioned, after I last saw you, I joined a mining group who own several operations across from the Almeda; over the next crest where "K.J." has his big operation. Well we aren't getting rich, but we've cleaned out the old entrance and cut another tunnel that has been producing enough that the three of us that have been spending the most time here are making enough that we may skip the logging this year and work it steady.

I told "K.J." that I was going to send you this letter and see if you want to put it in that book he said you were writing. We have seen the same kind of animal Bill said wrecked his camp. One of my partners was the first one to the mine this month after the BLM let us back in, and when he opened the chain on the upper road, he saw a large, brown two-legged critter climbing up the slope above the adit and into the pines. When he pulled his pickup alongside the storage shack, there were fresh tracks around it that he said were very big and the clearest print was huge. The weird thing was that it only looked like it had four toes! By the time I got to the mine, the ground had thawed enough that even though he had covered the clearest print with a piece of cardboard to save it to show me, the ground had settled so all I could see was a really large print, but no details.

Since that time, we haven't been bothered, but each of us have spotted the ape man watching us at times, but from way above. It will notice when we spot it and then it quickly disappears. This has to be the same thing that Bill saw at the PYX mine, but it hasn't bothered us, but we try not to leave our camp unattended, and we securely lock our shed when we have to leave.

Sorry I can't make it more interesting, but it sure is a curiosity and I can assure you that Bigfoot or whatever you call it doesn't appear to care to make friends, but it's not really an enemy at this point.

Let me know if you publish my story! Write!

George H. ~ Josephine County, Oregon

DON'T CAMP IN BIGFOOT'S BACKYARD

We purposely picked a time for our camping trip when we could pretty much choose from any spot we wanted, and for that reason, we chose the very end of summer. My wife took her vacation from the bank, and since I am a self-employed plumber, I had enough work lined up for my crew that we could be comfortable being gone, as there was no cellphone reception within 15 miles of our spot.

We had found it quite by accident, as we believed this area to be privately owned, because it was adjacent to a private and secluded home that shared the same access road. The lake is small enough that it goes largely ignored except from the residents of the home up from the lake, there are only a small handful of visitors to the lake.

We were driving around the area looking for access to federal land and just happened to enter this road one day when the owners were headed to town, and we hit it off well enough that they had explained that the lake was actually surrounded by public property, but that most people just turned around and left when they saw the house and it appeared that the road was their driveway. The road actually went downhill after their driveway turned off. They purposely let the weeds and small shrubs grow without cutting, as they effectively hide the lake completely; unless you are in a vehicle like a 4x4 pickup and really stretch to see ahead, you'd never know it was there.

Most maps don't indicate that *Summer Lake* even exists, as topographic maps make it look like a swamp with a stream flowing into it. In actuality, the stream flows out of the small lake; which is a beautifully clear, spring-fed oasis with a depth of over 20 feet, so it's perfect for a quiet getaway and catching the occasional trout. While we first thought it would be swampy because of the rushes and cattails, we found it has a nice gravel shoreline around three-quarters of the lake.

Image by Reid Priedhorsky

We have been spending our vacations here on and off for over eight years now, however we have had some unnerving events for the last three trips. The adjacent property owners would not want their names mentioned, but they have had even more trouble. This year was the worst yet, and when my wife read about your request for Bigfoot encounters, we can truthfully say we've had some!

You will, I'm sure, hear from some friends of ours, as they bought your book "They Saw Sasquatch" and they said they met Doc Bashford whose stories you printed in it. Doc is the person they first called when he ran the "Bigfoot Cavern" restaurant and bar. We ate there often and I remember the nine foot high carved Bigfoot statue he had in the entrance. Since we had these encounters, we have joined you on Facebook on your "Sasquatch Watch" page, so we know what we have seen is the real thing!

Three years ago we didn't have more than a strange event when we had been on a hike in the neighboring National Forest. Upon returning to our camp, we found our tent had been collapsed; the stakes had been pulled up on one side, the screen flap at the entrance was torn and the zipper just pulled apart. A few of our snacks like bags of chips and protein bars had been ripped open and it appeared that they were chewed on.

Our first thought was that the dog belonging to the property owners nearby had come over the hill, and we continued to make that assumption until when we left at weeks' end, we stopped to say goodbye and when we mentioned this incident, they said their dog was confined to their property by the chain link fence that surrounded their house and outbuildings, and the rest of the acreage was surrounded by three strands of barbed wire. We all assumed it could have been a bear, as they had found bear tracks on their property in the upper meadows.

Then last year, we again made it to our favorite spot and it appeared that we were now about the only people to have been there since our last vacation. That time, we brought our new dog with us. He is a golden retriever and just loves hikes and running in the woods, but my wife has refused to allow me to train him as a hunting dog. Rocky had a great time there, of course the first thing he did was dive right into the lake; swimming in circles, diving down under the lily pads, and then climbing out and rolling in the grass. He was in heaven! The tough part was drying him off before he came in the tent at night, but he was enjoying himself so much, we learned to sleep with wet dog smell. We kept Rocky close to camp and often chained him to a tree when we wanted to relax without him running off.

On our second night, Rocky suddenly let out a loud bark and was stretching his chain to the limits. We tried calming him down, but he just kept snarling and growling toward the deep woods. We shined our flashlights all around, but saw nothing.

The next day, we took Rocky on leash and went into the woods at the place where he had been growling and barking toward, and with Rocky's nose to the ground, we walked around a football field sized area and at one marshy point we found a very large footprint. I mean really big! It had to be the biggest animal I had ever imagined. The print was over 18 inches long and at least six inches wide, and it had claws at the tips. We found three prints and we both assumed it had to be a monster bear! There are only black bears in the state and we know they don't get that big.

We decided it was too dangerous to stay at our campsite any longer, so we packed up and went home that afternoon. As usual, we stopped to say goodbye to our friends and they said their dog had also been barking and excited the night before, so they kept him in the house. They said they thought they heard Rocky as well, but the distance was too great to be sure. Whatever it was had disturbed both dogs.

Well, this year we again decided to take a few days to get away and right back to our special lake we went. On our way in, we stopped to see our friends that live by the lake, and they came out to tell us they had experienced a break-in to their shed in back where they stored tools as well as canned vegetables and berries. Something had torn the door off its hinges and many jars had been smashed, but nothing was missing. The sad part was that their large sheepdog had disappeared. They said that they had left Barney in the shed when they went to town for supplies, and they figured that he had chased away whatever had broken the door and hadn't come back yet. We said we'd watch for him and headed to our campsite.

From the minute we pulled up, Rocky was acting spooked. He didn't run around barking, but just growled and slunk around as we set up camp. The whole time we were unpacking, putting up the tent and getting set up, Rocky just stayed close and occasionally just uttered a low growl toward the dark forest that surrounded the lake. Rocky stuck right by us and wouldn't even eat his dogfood. He did take a couple of hot dogs, which he quickly gulped down, but he just kept watching the woods.

As the sun went down behind the heavily forested mountain, Rocky suddenly jumped up, ran about four steps and started barking at something dark moving at the opposite shore of the small lake. Whatever it was couldn't have been a bear, unless it was actually walking through the marsh on its hind legs, which the game warden later told me was near impossible!

By now we were all alarmed, so with my wife holding Rocky's leash, I moved about a hundred feet toward the shape and fired my .357 magnum revolver into the ground. At first, the beast didn't move, so I fired again, and then it just slowly walked back into the trees; apparently not frightened as a human or normal animal would be with those explosions.

That did it for us! We came home the next day and reported this to the Forestry Department, but the person who we spoke with simply said, "Yes, we have heard about that particular creature, but we don't have the manpower to investigate every time we hear one of these stories."

Name withheld ~ Minneapolis, Minnesota

DROP THAT DEER OR I'LL SHOOT

This happened to me during deer season back in 2009. I was hunting in the valley between Bolan Lake and Tanner Lake. It must have been around 8:00 in the morning and I was wishing the sun would come out, as I had been at my chosen spot since 6:00, after tramping through ankle-deep snow. I was sheltered between a pine tree and a rock outcropping when suddenly my dream buck appeared across a shallow gorge.

Tanner Lake

I got my shot off and the buck just dropped cold! It didn't move, so I slipped my ought six over my shoulder, got my bearings, and dropped down into the valley between the peaks. I had marked my location carefully, as things look different when you change altitude; as you know. It must have taken me about 25 minutes to climb down and across the small valley and up the other side near Tanner Lake.

Well, I found the spot, but no deer! There was only a large red stain in the snow and footprints heading toward East Tanner Lake. It looked as if another hunter had got there ahead of me and stole my deer.

I was infuriated and I tore through the snow, which was only about eight inches deep, on the trail he had left. I was certain that it must have been another hunter, and from the tracks; I assumed it was someone with snow shoes similar to the short "Bear Paws" I had on, since the tracks lacked the tail that the longer snow shoes leave behind their tracks.

I was only 25 years old at the time, and being in good physical shape, I was really moving when I burst through the trees into a small meadow, and there running through an area of smaller evergreen was my deer! It was on the shoulder of what looked like a big man in a dark fur coat, but without any blaze orange that most deer hunters wear for safety; like what I had on. I was furious, and I unslung my rifle and triggered a round into the ground and I yelled, "Hey, drop that deer!"

That's when I almost crapped my pants. The thing turned back toward me and grunted like a bear. It looked like a monster ape, or else the ugliest person I had ever seen, and it shook its arm at me and made a kind of grunt. It seemed to be about eight feet tall and large-bodied. I stopped and just stared; not knowing whether to shoot it or run. The beast made up my mind for me, as it made a sort of a growl and turned abruptly into the forest; with me simply standing there with my mouth hanging open! I pulled myself together and ran after it, but I had lost precious seconds, and even though I followed as fast as I could, I finally couldn't even hear it anymore as it outran me. Well, I guess I actually saw a real Sasquatch!

Red Butte Wilderness Area

Just for fun, I am attaching a picture of Happy Camp's own Bigfoot. It is a metal sculpture that was created out of scrap metal by people that live there.

I'm sorry it is not a larger picture, but I took it with my cellphone which is pretty old. I also wanted to tell you about our annual Bigfoot Jamboree; it takes place every Labor Day weekend; it's fun for everyone with a salmon barbeque, a pancake breakfast, a parade and dances.

A.B. ~ Happy Camp, California

EVEL KNIEVEL'S FATHER MET ONE

My good friend Nic Knievel (Evel's brother) told me this story years ago and it may explain why the sons were so outgoing and daring in their lives. It had to be in their genes.

When they were young growing up in Montana, Bobby (Evel), Nic and their sisters must have had some exciting times. Nic told me stories that were too wild to be made up; they had to be true!

One of Nic's stories I remember well went like this: "Dad was a Fiat car dealer in Great Falls, Montana. One time Dad had caught a young black bear in one of his cage traps and on a Sunday when car dealerships were closed, as a joke, Dad broke in the back of the Chevrolet dealer's store, who was a friend, and let the bear out of the cage inside the dealership. Then he locked the store back up and went home."

I guess it caused quite a stir, but Nic said the whole town laughed about the tricks these guys played on each other. I can imagine the reaction when the Chevy people opened their store Monday morning!

Almost as a side note, Nic related another story that stuck with me from so long ago. He said that he had been out with his dad on their property one day when they spotted what his dad thought was a black bear, so he grabbed his rifle out of the pickup and they started around a hill so as not to be seen in their approach, and from the way Nic described it, they

34

walked over a mile down the small valley and when they came to the creek at the bottom, they turned and followed the creek upstream and downwind toward the forest where they had spotted the bear.

Nic said that his dad stretched up to peer over the tall grasses and then dropped back down and said, "That's no bear! You look, but be slow and careful." Nic said he peeked up over the grass and being shorter than his dad he had to take a couple of more steps to see it, and when he looked, its head suddenly turned and looked right at him. Then it turned up its head and acted like it was smelling the air.

Nic was quite the storyteller and he could really stretch something thin, but he got very serious for a moment when he said, "You know Gary: I've seen and done a lot of things in my life, but that time I was really scared and I know Dad was too." He went on to say that it seemed to be much larger than any black bear they had ever seen, but it walked on its hind legs, and when his dad looked again, Nic stood up with him and the animal had already travelled about a quarter of a mile, and as it reached the heavy forest, it looked back and then ran into the pines.

I remember when Nic told me this story that we were comparing our lives since we were the same age. Growing up in Montana must have really been an adventure that any kid would relish!

I was reminded of this story when I found some old papers where I had a note from Nic inviting me to attend the jump his brother Bobby (Evel) was making at Twin Falls, Idaho across the Snake River Canyon. Back then Bigfoot stories weren't the interesting topic they are today, largely I suppose, because of the difference in communication and news media from the 1950's and today.

From a story by Nic Knievel

THE BIGFOOT TRAP

My folks own property near the Applegate Lake in Southern Oregon, and although Dad always planned to build a summer cabin there, it seems that the closest any of the family ever came was taking a truck camper or travel trailer out to the place for a week or so at a time. My brothers and I have been taking turns enjoying the solitude of the beautiful forests, and a couple of times each year, we've been gathering to have a family reunion at the place. We're near the dam, but our property is not right on the lake, so we generally just take a boat or two with us when we go.

Applegate Lake

It's ironic that just a couple of miles from our property is the place where they built that large Bigfoot trap on Collins mountain.🐾 I guess it was built back in the 1970's; well anyway, somebody must have seen a Bigfoot again, because some people were up on the mountain searching for it. They came out of the woods behind our property and asked permission to cut back to the main road so they could get back to the campground where they were staying. They said they found some big tracks, but that was all. I didn't mention our experiences, because we don't need a bunch of strangers tramping around in our forests.

Anyway, about six months ago, we were making a routine check on the property to make sure our gate was still secure and that nobody had messed with the two aluminum boats we keep under the lean-to where our firewood is under tarps. There was still snow in the woods, so we left our rig parked at the gate and walked in so we wouldn't tear up our road with muddy ruts.

We weren't over a block in when we saw the tracks! At first we thought it had been a trespasser, but one of the prints was very clear on our road, and it wasn't human! Both my brother and I thought it might be a bear at first, but the tracks were too long, and besides bears should have still been in hibernation. These tracks were like a human giant with bare feet! The prints disappeared into the high grass, so the only ones we could measure were on the road and they were almost twice the size of my size 11 boots.

When we got to the sheltered area where the boats were, we saw more tracks that cut back around our lean-to and right behind the shed was a dead deer; a small doe that was torn in pieces. There wasn't much meat left, but there was hide and hair all over, and a huge gut pile and blood all over the snow; and there were those big tracks again all over the area! Some of the tracks were smaller, but they were still as big as my boot prints. It was like a couple of animals had killed the deer and then ripped her apart and made a huge mess. We left the gore there figuring coyotes or other critters would clean it up and we left.

Just as we got back to our pickup, a forestry truck came by and we flagged the driver down. It was a ranger that we were acquainted with and we told him what happened. He wanted to see the spot, so back in we went. He said several of the neighboring properties had seen a large animal back up in the hills that they said resembled a huge bear, walking slumped over and on its hind legs. He said their department put out notice to the staff that these incidents were not to be discussed because they didn't want a bunch of armed "nut cases" running around shooting at shadows. Supposedly, they had more reports from fulltime residents in the area of some bear-like animals doing damage, and even reports of missing and dead dogs. We had an abnormally cold and long winter, so they felt whatever it was must have run out of its normal food source. He took us to his truck and there under a tarp were the remains of a bobcat, and it looked like it had been ripped in half! He was taking it back to the Applegate office for more careful analysis.

It's very hard to get any of the BLM or forestry people to admit that this thing exists, but yet they all seem to be aware of it. What are they afraid of? Well, we keep hearing the same reports; I guess they just can't afford to acknowledge the information due to too heavy a workload. I have a feeling that the government knows more than they would ever admit to.

We'll let you know if any more happens.

E.B. Taylor ~ Applegate Valley, Oregon

🚶*Rumors of Bigfoot sightings came so often in this area that when a group of wildlife researchers from Eugene, Oregon went in search of the mysterious creature; they chose a site on Grouse Creek to build a trap to prove their theories and catch the beast that had everyone so fearful! In the early 1970's, this group constructed a solid wooden structure with heavy steel bars that seems it could hold a huge beast of a gorilla's size and weight. It was built upward from the Collings Trail on a spur not far off the main trail, and about 200 yards away. It was there that it sat for many years without any success except that it was rumored to have captured a hapless deer hunter for a time until he was eventually rescued. Finally, the state ordered the trap permanently disabled so as to protect the public and other wildlife from harm.*

Helping Wendy escape from the Bigfoot Trap

A FOOTRACE WITH SASQUATCH

I am submitting this story to you since it has lain since 1980, but I read your ad asking for actual sightings and contacts; so my wife encourage me to send it.

Back in 1980, I retired and my wife and I moved to The Dalles, Oregon. I was in a coffee shop one morning when I heard some guys talking about an Indian Racetrack over in Washington, so I checked with the U.S. Forest Service and got directions.

I went up in late Spring after the snow was gone, taking my White's Eagle metal detector, a knapsack full of goodies, including some bottled water, extra batteries and a camera. I was also carrying a canteen of water and a .22 caliber revolver. I went over through Carson, Washington to Forest Road NF6048. From there, I followed it to the trailhead parking spot. This is the southern part of the Indian Heaven Wilderness area.

The part that interested me most was the fact that historic records say that every year this area was used as a gathering place for the Native American tribes of Yakima, Klickitat and the Columbia River tribes, and they would meet to gather huckleberries. Thousands of people would camp there each spring and summer. This annual rendezvous was quite well known, and it was reported that the tribes had a horse racing competition. I heard that they placed bets on every race, and the racetrack had been worn several inches deep and straight as an arrow. One of the local old-timers told me that each tribe attending had side bets on all races and huge bets of goods and horses were waged.

Indian Racetrack ~ Image by Nwcamera1 - CC BY-SA 3.0

I figured it would be a great place to metal detect, so I set out to see if I could find artifacts; as it held more excitement than coin hunting in the local parks. I followed the trail through the forests and over mountain meadows and hills for several hours, and finally I came down into a beautiful area with two shallow mountain lakes and in between them ran a long, straight dirt trail that was the racetrack. It was about 10 feet wide and had to be about 2,000 feet long; at least! It was perfectly straight and without any grass or weeds in it.

Well, I set my pack down, slung my metal detector off my shoulder and started looking for any signs of old camps or anything showing where people had been. There were plenty of areas where there were clearings and evidence of where trees had been cut in the past, and in one meadow, there was a collapsed structure that must have been made by white men, because the rough timbers had the old square nails sticking out, but it obviously had been fallen down for a lot of years. I did find an old jackknife, but it was not recognizable due to excessive rust, so I placed it back where it had fallen; as it seemed fitting, and it had to be from a white man anyway.

The mosquitoes were horrible. Their stinging seemed more like needles as they attacked me without letup. In order to explore an area deeper in a forest of pines, I left my detector and knapsack alongside the racetrack at the northwest end and made my way through a particularly thick growth of balsams. I found a small pond where it seemed alive with frogs and tadpoles. It was filled by seepage from a slightly higher swamp which was full of cattails and grasses.

I was probably about two blocks away from my pack when I heard my metal detector chirp several times, but I didn't think much of it, because I assumed it may have slid on the grass; but suddenly it went off again only as it does when I'm swinging it over the ground as I'm searching. As I tore through the brush, I had thoughts that it may be another hiker, but upon getting back to the clearing, I found my detector laying by the trail and my pack was gone!

I ran back to the racetrack so I could get a view of the larger meadow and there was a creature! It was running fast down the racetrack and its gait was hard to explain; although it ran on two legs, it seemed more of a gallop, and it looked shaggy like a camel with that scruffy, loose fur hanging from it like it was molting. I yelled, "Stop;" and it glanced back at me as it abruptly cut off the trail into the forest! I didn't bother to follow it, because I couldn't ride a bike downhill as fast as that thing was going. I did look at its footprints in the sand and they were huge! I wear a size 10 hiking shoe and when I placed my foot on its print, it had at least six inches over my shoe. Fortunately, my pack only contained snacks, water bottles, and unfortunately, my camera. So I lost all except for my metal detector and the memory. When I told some friends about my experience, they asked me why I didn't shoot it, but as big as it was, I'm glad I never even thought about it; it might have torn me to pieces! I don't think an animal that large could be stopped by a .22 caliber. Besides, I was out of state, and it was not even human and I was in its home.

Even though I reported it to the forestry people at the time, I only got an, "Oh, Wow" out of them and the paper in The Dalles never did print anything, so it's all yours.🦶

Barry Rasmussen ~ Wasco County, Oregon

🦶 *Many submitters have said that they reported their sightings and experiences to the authorities, and their common response was kind of a, "We've heard it before, but we cannot officially comment."*

HUNTING WITH BIGFOOT

Thank you in advance for including my experience in your book. Due to company policy, I cannot allow you to publish where this location is, but as per our telephone conversation, I know you are familiar with the exact spot this happened.🦶

Ever since the federal government's war against our timber companies, this area has sat protected for over 15 years, and with the roads into these mountains being totally blocked, the effort to even try to sneak around, combined with the fines and penalties, isn't worth hunting or even hiking here.

I had been working around these mountains for years, and before the government closed it to hunting, I took some monstrous Roosevelt Elk out of these areas. Years ago, on a smaller ridge near a saddle, I got a shot at a huge elk with a trophy-size rack. He stumbled at the shot, so I knew I'd hit him, but he bolted back off the ridge into a dark valley. I followed the blood trail and reached a spot right between a huge boulder and an overhang with a ledge and a sort of cave underneath when I met what I thought was a devil from hell!

This monster had the huge bull elk over one shoulder and was just cutting around a large pine stump when it heard or smelled me, and it spun around and let out a combination of a scream and a growl, and I admit that I never before in my life was more afraid! Here was a monster ape-man covered with long fur, a huge dead bull elk on his right shoulder, and it was screaming at me. I tell you, I panicked; that elk had to dress out over 1200 pounds, and this monster was carrying it like a golf bag!

I took off on a dead run toward a fence that ran along the ridge and didn't even think about the rifle I was carrying. I only glanced back a couple of times until I got back to the six foot fence, and I didn't stop until I squeezed through a gap.

Once I felt I was fairly safe, being over a quarter mile away and behind six feet of barbed wire that I knew the monster couldn't squeeze through where I did, I thought it over. I was shaking; I couldn't even light a cigarette without leaning on the post. I suddenly realized I had wet my pants, but I felt anybody would have in this situation, so I'm not ashamed to admit it.

I did try to gather my courage, and started thinking about how famous I'd be if I could kill a Bigfoot! Finally I gave up, because I realized that the monster would not be standing still, it would be running away, even though it was three times my size and wouldn't have to run; I would have to chase it, and as the saying goes, "Chase it until it caught me." Instead, I went home!

Now that we will soon be logging this huge spot, I'm going to keep a careful eye out if my crew gets near that area; maybe I can find its home or at least meet it when I'm holding a chainsaw with a five foot bar. I'll let you know, and I'm packing a cellphone, so at least maybe I can get a selfie; ha!

Ralph P. ~ Northwestern Oregon

🦶 *This story happened at a spot we are quite familiar with and it is really kind of an eerie place. We hiked to it long before the government closed it off.*

Government restrictions, in order to save spotted owls, Persian butterflies and mythical fairies, have kept logging of our forests to a minimum which has led to jealously guarded secrecy of locations when a private logging company does get a contract. For this reason, and since we know this place, we believe this story to be factual.

WHAT IS THAT AWFUL SMELL?

I have been hiking various sections of the Pacific Crest Trail and preparing myself for a future goal to hike the entire trail from Mexico to Canada. Since I live in Oregon, it makes it easy to practice until I retire in four years. I have always enjoyed challenges like this and combining the beautiful scenery with an endurance test has been my dream for several years.

I was hiking a section of the PCT last summer and I had a terrifying experience that shook me bad enough that I had to report it to the ranger district in Eugene, but the on-duty deputy told me they have heard a lot of hikers tell similar stories; however without photos and positive proof like a Bigfoot body, they are following a policy of "neutrality." So I asked him if their policy is to deny this creature's existence until somebody produces a dead body. He just looked at me over his glasses and answered, "You got it."

My friend at work told me he saw your request for actual encounters for a book you are bringing out, and he even talked to (name omitted), who said he has your first book "They Saw Sasquatch," so I bought a copy. Glad to see I'm not alone, even if I can't prove what happened.

I was on the PCT in the area of Three Fingered Jack Mountain on my way to Mount Jefferson, and my plan was to go all the way to Cascade Locks on the Columbia River. My hiking partner was still on her summer break (she is a teacher in Lane County) and we had planned this hike carefully. After three days of covering a lot of ground, we decided to make camp and spend a couple of days just relaxing and doing nothing. We were probably a mile from the main trail in a beautiful meadow surrounded by an evergreen forest of huge trees; they were so tall that they blocked out the views of the mountains around us.

Mount Jefferson ~ Image by Peter Tiegs - Portland, Oregon

Our camp was on a flat bench near a small stream that trickled down to a large meadow covered by a carpet of wildflowers. Several large elk crossed far below us and we just sat and watched them graze along, when suddenly we heard a screech that we first assumed was an alarm call from a bull elk that had gone ahead of the others. With that, they all fled downhill and into the heavy timber on a dead run. We didn't know if there was a hunter coming, and since we don't hunt, I don't know if it was even hunting season. We watched the meadow for a long time for signs of whatever spooked the elk, and finally we saw something moving along the trail the elk had taken. At first we thought it was a large bear, and we watched it cut across the corner of the meadow the way the elk had gone.

Although we first thought it was a bear, it seemed strange, as it was walking on its back legs, but then we realized that its front legs were shorter; more like a human in body structure, but larger. Then the creature lifted its head high and turned like it had caught a scent in the air; suddenly it looked directly at us and then it dashed into the trees!

We were both speechless and we just looked at each other. After a few moments, we agreed that we had to know; so leaving our packs at camp, I pulled out my 9mm pistol that I carry out of self-defense mostly from humans, as animals avoid people. Cautiously approaching the place we first saw the creature, we talked aloud to make sure that it knew we were coming, as it seemed it had been afraid of us when it ran. I was sure that we were more afraid of it, but we had to know! The place where it crossed the corner of the meadow and where the elk had run away was fairly devoid of grass and mostly short stubble; it seemed to be an established trail with both elk and deer tracks in abundance. There were several much deeper tracks atop the others and four large prints that looked human, except that they were huge and looked strange. The toes all looked the same and it was hard to tell if there were four or five toes, as the soil was damp and by the time we got there, the prints were filling with water and caving in.

We both decided that the fun had gone out of our adventure and we headed back uphill to our camp. The breeze changed and was headed up the valley toward camp when we smelled the most god awful odor you can imagine! It smelled like something rotten. Having once worked for a slaughterhouse for a major meat company, I had been familiar with the smell of rotten meat, but this was the most putrid stench I could recall ever having smelled in in my life.

My friend and I quickly packed up our camp and beat it back to the PCT and departed the area at a very fast pace. We met some hikers going south on the trail and related our experience to them, and they answered in chorus, "Bigfoot!" In no uncertain terms, they gave us the assurance that we had done the right thing by leaving the area, and since they were headed the way we had come, they said they were going to camp that night far from where we described our camp had been!

We find it hard to believe that our government agencies won't formally admit to the existence of the Sasquatch; so a least they can tell hikers and campers how to avoid it!

Stan Messerly ~ Eugene, Oregon

THE BABYFOOT BIGFOOT

My husband and I had heard about Babyfoot Lake; a beautiful, circular, mountain lake near the Illinois Valley in Oregon, and since we were in the Cave Junction area for a few days visiting relatives, we needed some time to ourselves, so we decided it would be nice to go there. We packed a picnic lunch, thinking we would spend some time at the lake relaxing since it was early enough in the year that it should be rather devoid of people, what with traces of snow still lingering in pockets.

As luck would have it, we were the only car at the trailhead, so we put on our backpacks, grabbed our hiking poles, and we started off on the trail. It seemed different than the written description and directions we had looked at on the internet, as we found ourselves leaving the small valley and climbing at a steady angle alongside a steep cliff. We finally realized that we must have missed the gentle trail that led to Babyfoot Lake. We had looked at maps before leaving the car and we knew there was a higher trail so we assumed that this must have been what we were on.

We figured that the steep trail must eventually meet up with the other trail to the lake, so we decided to stay the course since we could see boot prints had already been on the trail this season. Well, we began regretting our choice after another half hour, because we were still climbing, and at places, the trail was just wide enough for a person's foot; one in front of the other! The way down wasn't quite straight, but if you slipped, it was about 100 to 150 feet before a tree or bush or maybe a huge boulder would stop your fall!

Finally, we reached the top of a ridge and the trail continued through the remnants of a forest along the crest of the ridge. There were still many dead, blackened trees from the Biscuit Fire that raged through the Kalmiopsis Wilderness back in 2002 and burned thousands of acres across these mountains. We had watched a documentary about this tremendous fire and its ravages were still so visible; it must have been terrible. There were also signs of recovery; with young trees and small bushes growing, but they were dwarfed by the huge dead pines that covered the mountains like gray ghosts with their arms outstretched as if asking for sympathy. Many of them still had pinecones that had kind of burned right onto the branches.

Babyfoot Lake, Kalmiopsis Wilderness

We finally reached the very top of a ridge where someone had piled rocks to form a cairn, which at the time; we hadn't researched enough to know what it signified. Not far from this spot was our first sight of Babyfoot Lake, several hundred feet below us. The trail led forward, and looked as if it curved down and around the mountain to the lake; it seemed more like a jeep road as it was wide and rutted from what we could see before it dropped downward.

We decided to take a lunch break with an overview of the deep blue pool, so we settled on a couple of boulders and began to unpack our sandwiches and water and enjoy the beautiful spring day.

Suddenly, we heard a loud thump, and as we both turned, a large softball-sized rock came skipping along the ground past us and disappeared over the cliff. Knowing we were on the highest point of the ridge, we knew it couldn't have fallen; it had to have been thrown, and we both yelled at the same time. There was no response and not a sound, but the wind whispering through the pines. We yelled again, but without any response.

The angle the rock had landed and rolled forward indicated that it came from the trees just where the trail started downhill, and that meant that it had traveled over 150 feet through the air before it hit the ground. We both know that anything that could throw a rock that large, that far, had to be too big to fool around with!

We took the easy and safe route by packing up and heading back the way we had come. The hair was standing up on the back of our necks the entire way down the trail, but we didn't hear or see anything further. By the time we got to where the lower trail was visible, we had both lost our interest in visiting the lake for now, so we made our way back to the parking area and were comforted by the sight of our car.

Jane Olson ~ Reno, Nevada

THE GUARDIAN OF BROWNTOWN

My family and I had recently moved to Merlin, Oregon and we have an interest in exploring. Coming from the Sacramento area in California, we really never had seen any actual gold mining areas, so our first quest was to find the ghost town of Browntown. We thought there would be some signs of it, but the people at the Holland Store said it was all gone; they went on to explain that in the 1970's some hippies from Haight-Ashbury in San Francisco had moved into the area and started a few communes and that they had torn down and taken every scrap of material they could to build their houses; mainly shacks from what locals say. Boy, they were sure correct; every sign of civilization was gone!

We did wander around in the place we knew it had been, but there wasn't even a foundation or anything there. We spent a couple of hours along Althouse Creek and had a picnic lunch in the flat meadow where we felt the town had sat.

So then we walked across the road and started climbing the steep hill. Just before leaving the Holland Store, we had also asked about a cemetery that was supposed to be on the other side of the road from Browntown that the gold miners had used, but they said they had never heard of one, so we got the hint that we weren't welcome to snoop around. Historic records indicate that the cemetery had been placed on the hill, as a place where it was not practical to search for gold. We knew that only the Caucasian graves would be there, as the

Chinese always exhumed their dead and sent the remains home to China so their people could achieve divine rest.

Althouse Creek

This large, steep hill was covered with the thickest brush we had ever seen. The blackberry bushes grabbed our clothing and made it difficult to get away. We tried to weave through it, while all the time looking for any sign of graves. Our kids are pre-teens and they kept wandering off even though we had all been warned about poison oak in the area.

At a point where we found a fairly open spot amid the trees, we felt that it would be a good place where pioneer miners may have chosen to place a graveyard, but we hadn't found any markings to indicate a memorial of any kind.

Our son came running up then and said, "Daddy, the scary man is watching us!" He pointed toward the trees further up the hill, but I didn't see anybody. Just then our little girl screamed something about a "big monkey" and came running and jumped into my arms. Looking around, I saw a large, dark shape that could have been a gorilla, but it ran when I spotted it, and the nearest thing I could compare it with was my first impression; a thin-bodied gorilla or a large orangutan.

It disappeared among a group of trees and I heard it crashing through the brush below. We all had enough of a look at it that comparing notes, we agreed it was about eight feet tall, stooped over, really hairy and with a face like an ape, but with hardly any long hair on the face itself. We walked the area where we had seen it and there was a large patch of ripe blackberries where it must have been eating. We found some loose hair that was clinging to a couple of bushes where it had run through on its retreat; the hairs were fairly long and straight.

On our way back to Merlin, we stopped back at the Holland Store and I was kind of reluctant to even mention what had happened, but we were pretty shook up by it. When I mentioned it, the man just nodded his head and said, "Yup, he usually comes down for the berries, but we think he lives up on the old Grass Flat townsite, and that area is closed off to people.

We just returned home then, but in researching, we find that Grass Flat was another gold camp above Browntown, but I don't know if it's really a good idea to go looking for strange beasts in these mountainous areas!

P. Nelson ~ Merlin, Oregon

🐾*Browntown was named for the first man to discover gold here, Henry "Webfoot" Brown, in 1852. It lies on the Althouse Creek near the present location of Holland, Oregon. A 17 pound gold nugget named the Collins nugget, after its discoverer, was found just about one mile above Browntown on the banks of Althouse Creek. It still holds the record as being the largest gold nugget ever found in Oregon. Nothing remains of the town or the other nearby settlements. The stories of Browntown's opera house, saloons, brothels, and the thousands of people, who passed through this area, are all that remain! Repeated successions of mining operations, hydraulic hoses and dredges over the years have erased even the remnants of the garbage dumps left behind.*

Browntown, a gold and copper mining town, on Althouse Creek in Oregon, just above the California border. This is the only known rendering of the town and was painted by Sigmund Heilner in 1865 as a Christmas present for Mrs. L. E. Hall, who owned and operated the hotel shown in the painting. Courtesy, HC.

SAVING BIGFOOT

Years ago (I won't go into exact details as to dates and years); I was paid a large sum of money to lead a party to a Bigfoot that lived near our farm. I backed out of this agreement when I found out I had been lied to.

I'll explain: For several years, we had regularly lost rabbits, chickens, ducks and occasionally baby pigs; we just blamed it on fox and coyotes whose population had slowly grown over the past several years. Since my dad had committed to work in Cloquet, Minnesota; my brother, sister and I were left to help our mother to maintain our small family farm.

One morning I went out to gather eggs and feed the chickens before going to school, and as it was still dark, I carried a battery lantern. As I neared the chicken coop, I saw a large shadow cut across the yard between the chickens and the barn. I dismissed it as my imagination, because there are always scary shadows of monsters and demons lurking about to attack kids who have chores to do around a farm.

As I came around the corner though, I saw a chicken egg between the fence and the chicken coop; I knew that something had been carrying that egg and dropped it when I approached. I held the lantern high in the air to shine over the yard and I saw something dark by the pasture fence. It was near the wooden gate that led to the cattle pasture. I yelled out, because I thought it might be the neighbor's kid who lived about a mile away, but it just leaped over the fence without climbing up on the rails. My light didn't allow me to focus, but I knew that this could not possibly be my neighbor, because it looked to be bigger than my dad, and besides, the woods between our farms was almost impossible to walk through in daylight, let alone in pitch black!

I walked back to where I saw the egg, and there were three large footprints in a muddy spot in the yard; they were very big, so I just figured that the thief had been wearing rubber boots like we always wear around the farm. I went into the chicken coop to gather the eggs and there were only four, when our hens normally would have over a dozen. The hens seemed agitated and weren't interested in their feed, and the rooster was up high on a rail scolding me. I told my mom about it and warned her not to go outside without the dogs just in case.

After school that day, my brother went with me to see if we could find out where this guy went. The ground was soft, as Minnesota fall days seldom warmed up enough to dry, and we found several footprints where this visitor had gone up our pasture road, which was little more than a mowed trail for our tractor and hay trailer, and the prints were hard to make out except for one in a grassless spot that was a real shocker. It was a bare footprint that plainly showed a huge big toe and four smaller ones. My brother just grabbed my arm and said, "Come on Johnny, there's a wild ape here and I'm going home!"

When Dad got home that night we told him, but it had rained and was dark, so he just dismissed it and said to keep an eye out for anything else out of the ordinary.

One night there was a program on television about Bigfoot hunters and it featured a sighting in Minnesota and gave a phone number to call if you had a sighting, so the next day I called. They sent a person out to visit our farm on a Saturday and I showed them where the footprints had been; we walked out through our pastures, and when we got way back in the woods near a large swamp, the man got really excited when he found a large footprint and signs of a lot of trampled down grasses and patches of brush piled up like it was to keep people out. They made Dad an offer to pay a sizeable amount of money upfront, and if they found a Bigfoot, a bonus would be added. Dad just said it's Johnny's discovery, so go ahead and he can be your guide.

We set the times during clear fall weather, and these people arrived with two vehicles and four people in the team. I opened the gates so they could get their 4x4s to the back of our 180 acre property, which was bordered on the back with a swamp covered by a huge forest of Tamarack trees and brush too thick to even hunt partridge in.

Then, these people started unpacking cameras, lights and guns! I asked them why all of the guns, and they just dismissed me by saying that since they were after an unknown creature, they were only to scare it away if necessary. They began setting up listening posts and built a few elevated platforms by nailing boards to trees to climb up, and then they made some small platforms above the high brush levels of the forest.

The third day, as I arrived at their camp a bit ahead of schedule, they were just sitting around a campfire drinking coffee and smoking, and they didn't hear me coming when I heard them discussing how famous they would be if this panned out. Then one of them said, "I just want to kill one and I'll be a rich man!" They all seemed to agree that this would be the best proof of all. Then, as I stepped on a stick, I was seen and they quickly changed the subject.

That afternoon we were deep in the back of our property and following a well-used animal trail. I was the last person in line, and I was lagging well behind the others, as I was suffering deep disappointment and feeling betrayed, when suddenly off to my right were two ape-like, shaggy brown creatures. They had just entered a small clearing when we spotted each other. We stared at each other for a few seconds, and then they turned and fled the way they had come. I went to the place they had disappeared and looked inside the dark forest under the umbrella of tall Jack pines on a large knoll. I saw the creatures again, and they looked back at me before going around a large root ball from a freshly felled tree from the last storm.

Just then, I heard a shout from the search team and they came running with cameras ready. The group said they had heard something running and figured they saw something; two of the party had guns in their hands. I don't remember how I responded, but it was something like; "Yeah, I heard it too and came face to face with two white tail deer." They ran off into the brush; and I pointed the way the creatures had come from when we first met.

For the next two days, I steered the party in the opposite direction from where the ape people had gone, and whenever they came close to exploring toward that downed tree, I discouraged them by warning of areas of peat bog that would suck you down like quicksand! Finally they left, and we didn't get any bonuses, but I have always felt good about saving those two creatures.

Over the years, I often think back to that moment and I'd imagine that the adult was a female, as it was about 6 feet high and the smaller one I'd guess was maybe 4 feet, but it acted like a human child; glancing up at the adult after it saw me and taking its hand. Anyway, I've waited a long time to tell my story, but I could not have lived with having been responsible for the death of such a rare creature.

Since that time, we have still lost an occasional chicken, pig, duck or eggs, but I have inherited the family farm now, so I can accept my losses knowing it's for a good cause!

Jon S. ~ Kettle River, Minnesota

THAT REALLY STINKS

I took a weekend trip to the Uinta Mountains to scope out a good place to go bow hunting this fall. It had rained the night before, so I knew I'd have the area to myself. I was walking along a trail that led steadily downward toward a creek when I came to a flat saddle that created a large forested area between two canyons. It was less than a half mile across, but it offered a beautiful plateau covered with aspen and an assortment of pines; reaching heights that must have topped out over 100 feet.

Kings Peak, Uinta Mountains ~ Image by Hyrum K. Wright

Suddenly, I was hit by a horrible odor. I had never before smelled anything so foul! It's hard to describe, but it was just sickening. However, rather than turn away, I could envision a rotting deer or elk that maybe possessed a magnificent set of antlers that would certainly be a treasure.

I tried to go toward the stench, but every turn I made seemed to diminish the intensity. As I took various turns, it seemed as though the smell was coming from different directions. The breeze was very slight, so it was really hard to fix a direction.

I wound around a group of huge trees and cut a trail that had fresh tracks of deer that were very clear and had not yet begun to fill with water from the surrounding saturated ground. Then I decided to follow them deeper into the forested saddle as I had lost the scent that had been so foul. The trail led slightly downhill and then wrapped around a huge boulder field.

I felt that this was going nowhere and I was just turning back to retrace my path to where I left the main trail for this plateau when my nostrils were again assaulted with that horrible smell. I turned to my right, where the breeze was coming from, and there at the far end of the small clearing stood a huge brownish-black creature standing on two legs, and it was looking at me!

I didn't know how to react; whether to run toward it or beat it out of there. The creature looked like a large bear, but with it staring at me, I couldn't see its facial features as it was partially obscured by a small balsam sapling, but it appeared larger than me, and all I had for protection was a small .380 pistol. It was hardly a match for a bear, so I simply froze, and the creature made my decision for me. It turned on a dime and was gone!

There I stood; not having the wherewithal to grab my cellphone to chance a photo or the common sense to do anything but stare in the direction it had gone. Gathering my composure, I then ran quickly to where the animal had stood, and there behind the sapling were two human-like bare footprints. I quickly made my way down the trail it had used, but I never got another glimpse of it and just heard a faint sound like a tree branch snapping and nothing more.

I returned to the last place I had seen it hoping to at least get a good photo of the tracks it had left, but they had been obscured by the surrounding mud, so I ended up with a picture that wasn't even worth printing.

Just before it started raining again, I returned to where I had started from, having come to the conclusion that what I had encountered had been a Sasquatch and that it was about seven feet high, had about size 18 feet, lots of brownish hair, and smelled rotten!

Now when I venture into the mountains, I have a camera, but I don't suppose I'll get another chance, and that really stinks!

Anonymous ~ Kemmerer, Wyoming

BIGFOOT STOLE MY BACKPACK

I hiked to Tanner Mountain↟ late last spring with the intention of capturing some unique photos. I had to wait until late spring to get back in and the trail to Tanner Mountain was still blocked enough in places that I had to break through hard packed snowdrifts covering the trail in spots, but it was a beautiful, sunny day.

I had to be extra careful in climbing this very steep trail, but the sun had cleared the slope for my assent. The last hundred feet or so is hard enough in summer, but there were still slick spots, so I took out my camera and mini tripod, leaving my backpack just below the large, dead snag that stands as a lone sentinel on the mountain.

Being extra cautious, I made my way to the crest, where in summer the blackflies totally cover the peak and they start biting 25 feet from the top. I could almost feel the little varmints as I got down and carefully crawled the last few feet and ever so carefully peeked over the top, so if there was a photo-op, I would capture it.

Crawling on my stomach and knees, I had my camera ready as I inched my out-of-shape frame up so I could scan the lake below. East Tanner Lake is not visible from where I was, but raising up carefully, and hoping for a prize winning photograph, I slowly surveyed the area and saw two black-tail does, and watched as they took one of the well-defined trails around the lake to an open spot near the far shore, but I couldn't see the bear or coyote that I had hoped to catch a shot of. I must have laid there in the warm sun for over a half hour hoping for a lucky break, but outside of a few crows and a couple of squirrels, nothing! I decided I'd retrieve my pack and just sit there and enjoy the hot coffee in my thermos and wait for the forest denizens to start milling around.

Looking down at Tanner Lake from atop Tanner Summit

I carefully backed down, so my standing up wouldn't alert the mountain forest critters to my presence. I left my camera on its tripod, as I had set it up to be focused on the lake, and with the remote switch on, it was ready to capture a winning photo, and all I had to do was trigger it by pushing the button.

Tanner Mountain Summit

If you've been on Tanner Mountain, you know how the safest ascent sort of curves around and wraps in a sort of spiral, so I carefully turned to my right and followed the trail as it looped around the dead tree that probably was alive when the Mayflower made landfall. As I made the corner and dropped below the tree, I saw my backpack; it was running through the large meadow about five hundred feet below me and it was in the hand of a huge, hairy, ape-like thief!

I stood there with my mouth agape watching an ape! It was running diagonally across the huge mountain meadow, and here I was, watching an animal steal my pack while my camera sat on the peak looking the other way! I quickly grabbed my S&W revolver and fired a shot into the snow beside me, and the critter really increased its speed, but it never looked back at me; it simply dashed down the trail and into the forest.

I know it seemed bigger than a man, and on my way back down the mountain, I saw where its tracks left the human trail and followed an obvious elk and deer trail. I did follow its trail a ways in hopes that it may have tossed my pack aside, but I finally gave up. It's so strange to finally see a mysterious being that so many of us have seen, but not even a photo to prove it.

I decided I would finally tell my story when I heard about your book. At least now I can join with others who know these things really exist.

Ted Barnes ~ Medford, Oregon

🦶 *Tanner Lake and East Tanner Lake, as well as Tanner Mountain and Tanner Creek were all named after Ezra Sherman Tanner, an Illinois Valley farmer turned gold miner. On many maps these places are shown as "Tannen" rather than "Tanner"; this was due to someone's error many years ago. A descendant of Ezra Sherman Tanner is working to get this corrected on maps and signs.*

UNIVERSITY PROFESSOR STEPS BACK IN TIME

I am responding to your "Sasquatch Watch" Facebook page and am submitting my own experience for your upcoming book.

This event happened when I was still a law professor, and the university would not have approved of one of their faculty reporting on such a controversial subject, so I kept it to myself until I saw your offer.

This incident happened to me and my wife Penny back in 2008 on a camping trip in northern Idaho, and for years, I've wanted to tell someone besides my close circle of friends. It's good to see that there are others who have had the same thrill of discovery, but at the same time, it's too bad that we can only share it safely with those who can believe in it, because we have all shared the experience!

Penny and I had always wanted to camp somewhere that was so remote that we could realize total privacy, with only the forest dwellers to share it with.

To experience this solitude, we wanted to find our adventure in a truly wild area, within sight of civilization, but only from a long ways up. We traveled to Idaho's Lake Pend Oreille.🐾

Lake Pend Oreille ~ Image by Scott Costello

The place we had chosen to begin our adventure was off of Lakeview Road and we parked our vehicle on a remote curve on this road where we could pull off far enough behind some pine trees so as to be totally hidden from the road. Then we loaded up two monstrous backpacks and headed into the Coeur d'Alene🚶🚶 National Forest in the direction of Echo Bay off of Bernard Point. We had stayed overnight in a motel back down the highway, so as to get an early start, and with many rest stops to accommodate an out of shape law professor, we spent the long summer day hiking northeast until we found a place suitable for an overnight camp.

The next morning we arose to a loud rapping sound that we assumed must have been a woodpecker working on a tree full of bugs. That was a suitable alarm clock, so we prepared a quick, cold breakfast, packed up our gear, and then headed through the heavy and deep forests again toward the lake.

By mid-afternoon we had selected our perfect camp; a flat, grassy spot surrounded by a beautiful evergreen and oak forest, with a stream of sparkling water running alongside a tent-site that seemed to have been created just for us! We cleared the area, put up our tent, and dug a latrine down below our camp in a small circle of young pines. To reward ourselves, we took a short hike up to the peak in order to view the lake; Lake Pend Oreille is the largest body of water in Idaho.

That night as we were relaxing before a picturesque campfire, we again heard a distant rapping; only this time we knew it could not have been a woodpecker because the sun had set and it was already pitch black in the inner forests. The sound was like someone smacking a baseball bat on a hollow tree, which I have done before; it's a sort of deep, reverberating sound. The noise would consist of a half dozen or so raps and then silence for a time, and suddenly, there was an answering series of similar sounds way off in the opposite direction from where we were at.

It was unnerving, but we weren't frightened, we simply had a sense that someone or something was communicating; like a mating ritual or something. Penny and I discussed possibilities which ran the gambit from bull elk claiming the territory, and even to the possibility of a group of the type that had established a neo-Nazi encampment near this area years before, but had finally been run out by the federal government.

There are some very remote areas in northern Idaho, and at least we knew that humans could not navigate these forests without light, so we could at least rest knowing that only animals could come close, and bear or cougar would likely stay away from humans. Not hearing any more sounds other than an owl and the far off howls and yipping of what sounded like a pack of young coyotes, we slept peacefully.

Next morning we woke with the sun and stepped out of the tent to greet the day, but something was different! The coffee pot was not by the fire-pit; it was laying under a large tree, and my backpack had been removed from the stub of branch on the large fir tree that I had hung it on. We found it down the hill below camp and behind a thick stand of blackberry bushes, and it had been opened. The zippers had broken, as if someone had just pulled it apart without using the zipper. The contents had been removed as though someone or something without knowledge of zippers and fasteners had used enormous strength to rip it apart! Several of the MRI (meals ready to eat) packets had been torn apart; the contents poured and scattered about, and it was like a big, strong creature had been carelessly inspecting the contents. A bag of marshmallows was torn open and it appeared that most of them had been eaten or carried off, but the torn bag remained.

After we cleaned up the mess and prepared breakfast, I went to the stream to fill the pot that we boiled water in and Penny visited the latrine, when on her way back she yelled, "Paul! Come over here and look at this." When I got to her, she was leaning over a spot in the creek just staring at the sandy shore by the water's edge. There were two huge footprints that appeared to be about one and a half times larger than my size 11 ½ hiking boot! The prints looked human, except for the obvious claw-like marks at their tips.

We had heard of Bigfoot before, but like most people, we casually dismissed the reports as most likely bears and wishful thinking of "wannabe adventurers." However, this was different. It really had happened and to two fairly educated people; Penny is a high school principal. So there we were trying hard to rationalize a bear that left large humanoid footprints, and that lifted my backpack quietly off a tree branch five feet high, and went through it with us only 20 feet away!

Well, we cleaned the area up and stayed close to camp all that day rather than hike up to view the lake again. Later that afternoon we heard a series of raps again that sounded like whatever it was, had moved closer to our camp. Still later on, we were startled by an even louder series of beats, and they seemed a lot closer to us! By this time we had begun to feel most unwelcome, and we reached a point where the enjoyment of nature had lost its appeal, so we warily camped again that night and the next day found us rapidly hiking back to our vehicle.

Our GPS unit returned us to the welcome sight of our car, and we heaved a sigh of relief when the engine started immediately; we had been concerned about that, as we were really anxious to just get out. Then, as we were crawling along our meandering trail back to the gravel county road, a creature darted across the road about 50 yards ahead of us, and we both concluded it had to be a bear running on its hind legs. Then we ruled out that possibility, as it looked too much like a large ape, but it didn't seem to have a neck. We hadn't seen it for more than seconds, and it was angled toward us, so the shock of it seemed to blur our memories.

We never spoke much about this incident, and only to a very close circle of friends; usually we kept it light, to leave room for the ribbing that always followed, but we had experienced something that compels a person to want to share it.

Then, as it happens, in July of 2010, a fellow professor invited me to accompany him to a "Sasquatch symposium" in Oregon which was chaired by the well-known anthropology professor, Dr. Jeff Meldrum from Idaho State University. Dr. Meldrum's presentation was most interesting, and I came away knowing that I finally had the answers. As far as "no neck," Dr. Meldrum explained that the Sasquatch actually has seven cervical vertebrae, but appearance would suggest that is has no neck because its massive skull is highly mounted.

Now that I am retired and have the time to explore, I no longer have the desire to chase out to find this elusive beast, but as I enjoyed the encounters you published in your last book, hopefully your new readers will enjoy mine.

Dr. P. Farnham ~ Tampa, Florida

🥃*Pend Oreille is pronounced* **pond oh-ray**. *The following information comes from the website boisestatepublicradio.org: The French name comes from fur trappers and it means "hangs from ears." That comes from the round shell earring worn by male and female Pend d'Oreille/Kalispel tribe members. To further the confusion, Idaho also has a town called Ponderay, and there's a Montana county called Pondera, all with the same pronunciation.*

🚶🚶*Coeur d'Alene is pronounced* **kore-duh-lane**. *The following information comes from the website boisestatepublicradio.org: Coeur d'Alene is the name of an American Indian tribe who lived in the area and called themselves the Schitsu'umsh. They got the name Coeur d'Alene, which means "heart of an awl," from French-Canadian fur traders.*

A TALE FROM TABLE MOUNTAIN

My Sasquatch encounter took place almost 25 years ago, but the memory is still very clear. In 1992, I relocated to Idaho Falls, Idaho from San Diego, California, and the following spring I was having lunch with several of my coworkers when someone suggested we hike the Table Mountain trail as soon as some of the snowpack had receded from the Tetons. He said it was a pretty difficult hike because of how steep it was, but we would be rewarded with the most magnificent view of Grand Teton. Four of us decided we'd take on this challenge.

Grand Teton in winter ~ Image by the National Park Service

I was used to running three to five miles every day on level terrain, so to get prepared for Table Mountain, I began to add running up and down the bleachers at the local high school, and by the time mid-June rolled around, I felt prepared to tackle the mountain.

Very early on the morning of our hike, we met at a grocery store in Rigby, so we could carpool to the trailhead. By now, there were six of us ready to hike. From Rigby we drove through Driggs and then to Alta, Wyoming. After that, we turned on Teton Canyon Road which took us to the trailhead.

It was a beautiful, clear day and it was promising to warm up nicely. There was a stream at the trailhead, but we knew that after that there wouldn't be any springs or creeks, so with that in mind, I was carrying four Platypus water containers along with a half-dozen protein bars in my daypack. I didn't know if that would be enough for an 11 mile roundtrip hike, but I'm very slightly built and didn't think I could manage more than that.

Right from the start the trail was tough going, and after the first mile, one guy said he just couldn't go any further and was going to turn back. The rest of us could hardly blame him, as he had broken a leg about six months ago, and gotten out of his walking boot only four weeks ago. Another hiker said he'd go back down with him; the rest of us thought this was a good idea, because his face had turned so red and we were worried about him going on.

The rest of us kept steadily climbing, and at about the three-mile mark we reached a large meadow and the first signs of snow. We could see snowpack ahead of us, so we stopped here for a break, and after having a snack and some water, we discussed whether we would be able to make it to the 11,000 foot summit. We decided to go up to the next crest and see just how deep the snow was. This turned out to be a steep and arduous climb, and we were all worn out by this time.

As we stood there talking about turning back, suddenly up ahead of us was a huge, shaggy bear! It was about a half mile away and headed in our direction. It was walking upright on its hind legs and growling. We could hear a high-pitched squeal that was being borne on the cold breeze retreating down the mountain. As the beast got a little closer, we knew it couldn't be bear; it didn't have any fur on its face, and the orangish-brown hair on its body was much longer than a bear would have. It raised one arm in the air and shook a big, meaty fist at us. That's when we all turned and ran.

We didn't say a word to each other all the way back down the trail. It didn't take us nearly as long to return to our starting point; it was all downhill and so treacherous in places, it's amazing that no one fell and broke their neck!

When we got back to the car, our two friends were waiting for us, and by some unspoken agreement, we didn't say a word about what we had encountered up there. When they asked us why we were back so soon, someone said the snow was too deep to make the summit, and the rest of us nodded our heads in agreement. It wasn't until someone asked me what happened to my backpack that I realized I must have dropped it when we started to run, and I certainly wasn't going to go back to get it.

I regret having missed out on the spectacular view of Grand Teton, as I remained in Idaho for only another year before moving on, and to my knowledge, not one of us ever mentioned what happened. This is the first time I have told anyone about my experience.

Anne B. ~ Salt Lake City, Utah

🏃 *The following information comes from the website www.greater-yellowstone.com/Teton-Valley: Table Mountain is a must do hike not to be missed in the Tetons. The top of Table Mountain offers the best vantage point in the Tetons for close-up views of the massive west face of the Grand, upper reaches of Cascade Canyon, and the U-shaped glacial valleys and canyons on the west side of the Tetons. This hike is widely regarded as one of the most outstanding in the entire region and it bears the signature of the essence of the Grand Tetons.*

INSURANCE COMPANY SAYS LIE ABOUT BIGFOOT

I saw your ad for Bigfoot occurrences and my wife and I have definitely seen one firsthand, and believe us, they exist!

Last October, we were just driving around enjoying the fall colors and having never been to the town of Powers, but always saw the road signs, so we were wandering around the roads trying to figure where we were, because Josephine County maps don't work at all when you suddenly find yourself in Douglas County. Anyway, after we stopped and asked a county work crew who were cutting branches near the narrow paved road for directions; we had just come around a sharp curve, and there on the hillside was this huge being, about a hundred feet up the hill on the right side of the car, and I pulled over because we both just couldn't believe it.

It looked like a large brown, shaggy humanoid; my first thought was early depictions of Cro-Magnon, but it had long hair, a face that had kind of short hair, and its arms were almost as long as its legs. It was moving fast uphill grabbing bushes and pulling itself up quickly. Then, I got the idea of blowing the horn to make it turn while Julie was digging in her purse for her cellphone, because all we could think of was to get a picture!

The minute I blew the horn, it whirled around and opened its mouth like it was yelling back at me, but the windows were up so we didn't hear anything, and then, just that fast, it lobbed a basketball-sized rock at us. It hit right on the corner of the passenger side of the windshield and it sent glass shards all over the place. I guess we were distracted and scrambling for long enough, that by the time we both recovered enough to look out, the thing was gone!

Well, that ended our fun trip, and we both got out my door, as the passenger door wouldn't open; we brushed out the seats as best we could, and found our way out of the maze of roads and finally ended up reaching Interstate 5 at Glendale, and then we headed south to home.

West Fork Bridge over the Umpqua River, Douglas County, Oregon

Monday, being the next day, I called our insurance agent and told him our story, and I could almost picture the look on his face by his reaction. I was all set to call the newspaper and make a big deal about it, but he told me he had run into these situations on a couple of occasions, and he said absolutely do not fill out the report as it really happened. He said, "I am not advising you to lie, but I strongly recommend that you just say a rock rolled off a hill and hit you." He went on to say that in one case the company paid the claim and immediately canceled his client's policy. In the other instance, the claim was paid, but due to the inquiries from the insurance company, the client's employer (a state agency) made the person go in for a series of examinations, including an immediate drug and alcohol screening. My agent further said the man was certain he lost the promotion he had been expecting because of this incident. We decided to report it as our agent suggested.

Now that I have a chance to share our experience anonymously, we can at least tell, what to us was the scariest, yet most exciting event ever! We have shared our adventure with close friends, who believed us, and another friend also saw this kind of animal, but we still want to remain anonymous.

Name withheld ~ Medford, Oregon

BIGFOOT JUMPED OUR CLAIM

I am employed as a teacher at a high school in northern California, and I have spent some time exploring the mountains on the California/Oregon border the last two summers. Coming up from the Bay Area, the real wilderness areas have truly been an adventure.

A fellow faculty member and I decided to try our hand at gold panning in the mountains above Happy Camp, California. We took my friend's truck and camper, and on the advice from local area authorities, we headed north out of Happy Camp.

We met a miner, whom we were referred to by a state employee, and he sold us the gold pans, shovels, trowels, and right down to magnifiers and tweezers; and he gave us a quick lesson on how to pan. Then, following his directions, we headed off for a new adventure!

For the better part of our first day afield, we spent our time driving on various roads, some of which were not accommodating to a large 4X4 pickup and camper. Long trips of backing up and reversing direction found us sitting by a small stream in an exceptionally dark forest where the sun sneaked away behind the mountains before we knew it, and even though we could look up to see light, we needed our battery camping lamps and our cozy campfire to comfortably see. We relaxed by the fire, had a few beers and roasted hotdogs and marshmallows like kids; looking forward to striking it rich on the morrow.

Early the next morning, we were awakened by a loud rapping that we joked was a "woodpecker alarm clock." After a hasty breakfast and coffee to take the morning chill away, as it was colder than we had prepared for; we spent a couple of hours trying to even find a way to get enough material in a gold pan to even be able to find any sand, let alone be able to look for gold. It seemed that the entire stream was just golf ball to basketball sized rocks, and we finally gave up and got back out to the highway; heading north until we saw a rather well-traveled dirt road heading east.

Grayback Mountain, Oregon~ Image by Bureau of Land Management Oregon and Washington

By now we likely were very close to the Oregon border, but it wasn't like anyone would care way up in these mountains. We came to a fork, and since we were looking for water, we took the road that headed downward. Down we went; the road curved first right, then left, and it branched off in different places, but we stayed on the main traveled part; and it was a well-maintained route, even though we never saw another vehicle. Finally we saw a stream, and it curved close to the road at one point where we could see a clear spot where someone had likely camped alongside a monstrous pine tree on our left side.

We pulled in and first checked the stream; it was perfect for what we wanted. It curved abruptly away and directly opposite of where we were and toward some rugged looking hills with a large mountain towering above this beautiful valley.

We totally unpacked the truck at this point; camp stove, coolers, and all of our other gear. We put some beer in the cold stream and set up camp; it was absolutely the thing dreams are about! We even built a fire pit, for aesthetics mainly, as we had a Coleman stove, and we even cut a couple of poles to erect a lean-to tarp. Then, after a little refreshment, we were ready to become goldminers.

Four hours later, we began to realize that the romantic notions of goldmining really had to be more dream than reality. Even with rubber boots, our feet were almost frozen. It is not possible to squat and pan gold comfortably. Even with hip boots, you still have to kneel down and water is bound to get in. Besides that, muscling larger rocks by prying, shoving, lifting, and prying again is hard on the back and legs. The process of first moving aside those largest rocks you can and shoveling and scraping up enough gravel to partially fill the gold pan, then picking out the large stones to get down to fine sand is a long and extremely tedious routine to get down to the real meat of it.

If I sound negative, don't get me wrong; it was exciting;

especially when we got down to the point of finding that treasure of black sand. Our instructors and advisors all told us, that is the key to finding gold! It makes sense, because the black sand is the heaviest and sinks to the very bottom, likely because there may be lead or whatever in it; all we know is that's the key.

Gold is even heavier, and finally, I found black sand, and I thought I'd hit the "mother lode" as they say! I carefully picked out the pebbles, and there across the bottom of my green pan was a bottom covered in black sand, and scattered among the black sand were about 20 pieces of gold as large as aspirin, but flat. I yelled to my partner who was downstream and he scrambled over to see my wealth.

I guess he must have heard something I missed, because the first thing he did was to crush my gold pieces with his fingernail; it just shredded in the pan, and I was introduced to silica! No gold, just gold colored flakes, that when crushed, are light enough to float on water. I was crushed as well! I had enough for one day, so we just built a campfire by the water, as it was cooling in the mountain valley even though it was still two hours before sunset.

The next morning, we were again awakened when it was still dark in the valley by a rapping sound. I said, "Looks like our woodpecker followed us." However, this was different; louder, a lot louder, like a heavy stick being pounded against a hollow tree. That was how both of us described it, but soon forgot about it. After breakfast, we were goldminers once more.

By mid-afternoon, we finally found some real gold! Digging

down on the downstream side of a huge boulder that covered half the creek, I was elbow deep and up close to my chin in water, but I was bringing up some really black sand. My first attempt found my pan almost half full of sand. I moved closer to the shore so I could kneel closer to the pan, and I carefully sloshed the contents back and forth, and now the yell I let out was real. I had found gold; many pieces with several as large as the head of a common straight pin!

My partner joined me in working deeper and wider all around this large boulder, and by the late afternoon we had half of the gold collector bottle full of gold; success as last! It was really a lot of work, but from what we had been warned about, we felt very lucky. That stuff is heavy! We knocked off early in the evening, tired from our exertions and turned in right after dark; we were both exhausted.

Sometime in the middle of the night, we woke to a crashing. Something had smashed against the camper. We both jerked awake, grabbed flashlights and bolted out the door with revolvers in hand! My partner had a .38 caliber and mine was a .22; never thinking we'd need them for protection, but now we were under attack.

Shining our lights all around the area, we saw nothing. Our camp stove was laying smashed alongside the camper where it had been thrown, and the side window was cracked and a chunk of fiberglass was hanging loose, so whatever threw it had a lot of power! We had two powerful search lights, but did not see a thing anywhere.

Neither of us could sleep after that, so we made a fire and sat there for two hours until dawn. Once it was light enough, we searched for signs of what or who could have destroyed our stove, and we found very large, bare human-like footprints all around the truck and down by the water where we had left our mining tools. The intruder had also taken a shovel and our pans, one of which we found way down the creek on the opposite bank; it was split in half, and that is exceptionally hard to conceive of, as tough as they are!

We took our guns and followed the gigantic footprints which led along the creek going downstream and then around a bend marked by a large, dead tree they disappeared. We figured that either it crossed the creek or went into the thick bramble and blackberry bushes that surrounded the huge tree. It was then that we heard a loud crash back at the truck!

We headed back on a dead run, slogging through the soft sand near the creek, as it was still a faster path than the razor sharp thorns and blackberries. As we approached, running as we could in our Birkenstocks (California dress shoes), and nearing the truck, we saw a large rock fly from the patch of bushes and pine trees about fifty feet from the truck; and this rock was the size of a basketball!

It hit the passenger side, smashing the door and shattering the window. We both fired our revolvers at the place the rock had come from. I think we emptied both guns, as I remember, because we were both reloading before we moved further. The passenger side door was totally crushed, there was glass all over the inside, and the rock was on the passenger side floor. I hate to admit it, but anything that could throw a hundred pound rock over 50 feet is more than enough adventure!

We got out of there as fast as we could get the mess scraped out of the truck and throw the rest of the gear into the camper, while watching warily for an attack. We hit the road and then we made a point to find our contact back in Happy Camp, and when we told him what had happened, he calmly answered that he should have warned us, but it's a little early in the year for any Sasquatch sightings, so maybe it may have had young nearby that it was protecting. He went on to say from our description, that the area we described was hardly ever visited by people, because the road ended about a quarter mile from where we camped. Looks like most people turned around and left, that's why it looked so used; I almost wish we had turned around also.

The good news, if just having the encounter of a lifetime was not enough, was we had the gold appraised at $480.00. We split it and are saving it as conversation pieces on our coffee tables; with our wives permission of course.

Name withheld ~ San Jose, California

TOWN AUTHORITY KEEPS TRACK OF APE CRITTERS

My husband and I were searching through great granddad Charles Grable's old diaries; he passed away back in 1946 and his diaries were so interesting that some of them were on display in the old Kerbyville house for a long time and then handed down to us. We saw these references to ape men and thought you might use this for the book the historical society said you were working on.

Charlie was a sort of postmaster for a while and we were told that he knew more than most people about the Illinois Valley, and many people would go to him for asking and reporting what was happening in the county. Not like a town gossip, but more like the central information recorder I guess. Anyway, the old articles appeared in the Argus Newspaper which soon became the Courier.

Granddad seemed to have a deep interest in the ape men reports and the ones we're sending you were in a separate binder; he kept a sort of diary of these events.

Publisher's note: Charles Grable's notes have been transcribed it exactly as written; with no correction to punctuation, spelling or grammar.

- June 1911 – J.C. Matteson of the Oriole mine in Galice said two of his men on the late shift reported a big ape-like beast pushing rocks down the slope as they came off shift. A big one hit Tom Rockwell's thermos and smashed it. The foreman just told them to forget it and not say anything. Ore bringing $210 a ton so making hay on both shifts.

- August 1914 - Sailor Diggings – Jayhawker Williams said he worked at Sailor Diggings (Waldo), and back in them days they had a giant two-legged critter stealing food from the cook shack. Said it must have been nine feet high. Nobody ever shot it, but he said it got scared off.

- July 1915 - Reported sighting of an eight foot tall forest critter with light black hair, but walked on two legs was seen near town.

- August 15, 1920 – Phil Haldsworth reported seeing one of the giant ape critters up on the B-level of the Almeda mine. This is the fourth miner to see one. It didn't do anything but watch him go to work. Phil said it was huge, but he was running late so he hurried by. Said he would have anyway, big as it was. They're finding copper, silver, lead and gold in the Almeda on all three levels.

- No date, just a notation – The owners of the Gold Bug mine; C Romig and Annie Neil hired Tom Mathers to sit guard at the mine site for a shot at the ape man if he comes back. He's been going into the supply shed and stealing potatoes and whatever else can be eaten.

Cindy L. ~ Cave Junction, Oregon

🐾 *The following information comes from the website Oregonencylopia.org: Kerbyville was named after James Kerby (or Kirby), who filed his original homestead in 1855. The Kerby post office was established there in September 1856, with James Kerby serving as the first postmaster. Kerbyville was chosen as the county seat in a county election a year later, beating out Grants Pass; but in 1886, as Grants Pass grew and became more accessible by railroad, the county seat was moved there.*

Kerbyville's name was changed to Napoleon in 1856 by the territorial legislature, perhaps because some thought that every Josephine (County) needed her Napoleon. This may have been the influence of a Dr. D.S. Holton, a principal landowner in the area and an enthusiast of Napoleon III and Empress Josephine. But the name was not popular and was changed back to Kerbyville. Eventually, the name was shortened to Kerby, as it is known today.

One of Oregon's oldest post offices is where the Kerbyville Museum is today. James Kerby was its first postmaster.

EXPLAINING BIGFOOT

I had a face to face meeting with an overly large and exceptionally spooky mountain monster, and I can now honestly say I met a Sasquatch!

I spent the last 15 years living on the Oregon coast, and although we moved here from northern California where the people are all not that different, the lifestyle is more relaxed here, and I have been able to hike in some truly wild areas.

I can see why this strange animal is seen and reported, yet still remains unknown, because it lives where most people would never go.

I would never have seen the one I did had it not happened that I sort of dropped in on it. Occasionally, I enjoy just going back in some fairly non-scenic place where I won't run into a constant troop of other hikers, photographers, exercise fanatics and kids. Having lived most of my life in and around population, sometimes it's nice to just be alone. To do that in the mountains of Oregon is difficult, because it's just too beautiful. So sometimes, I look for the seemingly unattractive areas in hopes I may find a an unusual rock formation, gnarly tree branch, or just maybe find something that four million other people haven't seen!

Well, this trip was even more than I could have bargained for. It was up on what is called Bald Knob, in area in the Rogue

River-Siskiyou National Forest. I had taken my old Willys up a road that was more of a trail, but not inviting I'm sure to most people, because this particular route was full of large sized rocks. I was up fairly high and I could see Humbug Mountain, but this area was just not anything that would draw visitors, so it was just what I was searching for. The road on the other side of this hill got worse, so I knew I'd have a private area to explore.

I parked off the ruts, and grabbing my pack, set off down into what looked like a really secluded canyon. The road soon ended, but there was a shallow gulch that led down to my left, and I found myself in a beautifully sheltered canyon that was virtually covered with pine trees. There seemed to be a well-traveled animal trail that kept steadily descending into this ever deepening canyon, so I figured I couldn't get lost by staying on it; so I spent about two hours following it.

I had to go quite slow, so I'm not sure how far down I was when I heard the sound of water splashing off to my right and it seemed like it was almost directly below me. Leaving the trail, I slowly climbed hand over hand over a couple of huge boulders laying on the steep slope, and the sounds got louder, and now I could see part of a small waterfall coming from the cliff on my upper right, so I carefully went around the huge boulder; I had to hold on to its side with my fingers, as my feet kept slipping on the steep gravel slope as I made my way slowly down until I was directly under the boulder, and then my hands could no longer find anything on which to hold, as the rock was too smooth! My feet kept slipping on the open stretch of gravel and then I lost it. I landed on my butt and slid on my back down about 30 feet at a fast pace, and then I dropped right off an abrupt edge and landed hard enough to take the wind out of me, but fortunately, I only dropped about three feet to where I thudded down; and there I sat, waiting for the stars to clear.

I had landed on a small ledge and below my outstretched legs the slope dropped down to a very steep funnel-like chute through a really bad-looking channel that was lined with huge rock walls; it looked like if you fell down that slope, you'd just have to keep going all the way to the bottom of the mountain! Fortunately for me, although I had a lot of pain, I wasn't broken. Gathering my senses, I looked around me and there on my right was a small pool that a trickling stream had been splashing into and then it flowed off the far corner of the five-foot pond and disappeared from view off the back side.

It was here that I saw the subject of my letter to you; bet you thought I'd never get to it! It's just that this was the most exciting event that ever happened in my life, so forgive me.

Over a huge boulder to the side of the pond and about 30 feet up, there was a huge, light brown haired head. It had an ugly face, to be sure by human standards; more like a large gorilla-like animal with rather large eyes and ears, a kind of flat nose with big nostrils and large, but flat ears. I couldn't see its hands or arms, so it had to either be laying up there or standing behind that large rock, but all I saw was this very calm but seemingly curious animal. I say that, because it had a smooth, dark skinned face, and its brow was wrinkled like an aging human would look.

Then I got courage, and very calmly said, "Hello." As nervous as I was, I was now more anxious at finding something I never believed really existed! Well, I guess I should have let it make the first move, because the animal, all of a sudden, rose up a couple of feet, turned and disappeared. All I saw was a lot of long hair, but the rest of its body was behind the rock. Then I heard a couple of thumps, like it must have jumped and ran downward; and then nothing!

I was not in good enough shape to try to climb up to where it had been, even if I had gathered enough courage, but I had scrapes and bloody spots all over me, and I was just very lucky to have not broken anything except maybe my butt! I have never had so many abrasions and bruises at any one time before in my life, and I carefully and painfully made my way back to the Willys. I think I must have taken three times as long to get home, and it took over a month for the wounds to fairly well heal!

You know, the funny thing about all of this, is my next door neighbor is a retired Oregon state employee and he happened to be mowing his front yard when I pulled into my driveway, and when he saw me slowly and painfully climbing out of my Jeep, he came quickly over. I told him the whole story and asked him who I should tell about what happened, thinking I'd at least make the news; he started shaking his head and told me I had better just forget it ever happened because no one would ever print it or even accept my story.

He wouldn't even allow me to use his name, as being a retired forestry worker, he was under a lifetime restriction against reporting, discussing, or even acknowledging the existence of the Bigfoot. As I stood there bleeding and suffering bodily, and now mentally, he explained that a great many of the BLM, forestry, and other state employees have seen and encountered these creatures, and the ruling about "nondisclosure and absolute denial," has been in effect ever since the first sighting was reported. The policy has a multiple purpose, and after hearing him out, I could understand the devastation that would occur if the state agencies admitted to the existence of these beings. The forests would be flooded with hunters, and shootings would be rampant; people would create such destruction that it would be chaotic!

After listening to his well-rehearsed presentation, I could see it was not his first recital, and I then understood why I too need to respect what I had experienced. I did go back to my neighbor again, even though it's been so long after my encounter, when I decided to answer your request for Bigfoot experiences for your new book, and he said as long as I didn't reference our previous conversation or use his name there was no problem. I showed him this letter and he wants to read my story again when the book is published.

Anonymous ~ Brookings, Oregon

GRANDPA'S RECORD OF BIGFOOT RUMORS

Publisher's note: This submission has been transcribed exactly as written; with no correction to punctuation, spelling or grammar.

We saw your "Sasquatch Watch" page and your request for Bigfoot stories, and recalled an interesting note in my grandfather's diary. Grandpa kept a series of diaries that he kept on an irregular basis, simply dating and recording on the pages of a leather-bound notebook. When we read your posting, we remembered this book and thought you'd find this entry interesting. I hope you can read this, as I just laid the open book in our copier.

Grandfather worked at a mine called the "Alameda. 🚶

June 9 1922
Had some excitement at the mine today. Some of the boys been talking bout goin off on there own and finally they done it. Hope they strike it rich

Our foreman warned the rest of us not to try it cuz we'd never work anywhere again. I been thinkin of goin myself but I'll wait and see it they get rich first.

June 22 1922

Sure glad I staid here after all, cause the search party found Jim Lowell alive and two of the boys they culdn't recognize cause they was torn to peaces. Heads were torn off so they buryd the bodys there on the riverbank and never found the other guy. Don't know who is missing cause they couldn't tell whose bodys they did find they are still working on it.

Heard that they was attacked by apemen and the search party said there was big monster sized footprints all over. Figured on talkin with Jim cause they sed he was comin back tomorrow.

June 23 1922

Jim never came back and we had a meeting. The bosses said nobody had better try that agin! I thought mebee the bosses told us that awful story to keep us from quitting but a couple of the searchers said it was all true.🦍🦍

Old man Rainy🦍🦍🦍 told me he heard about an ape creature when he was working at the Lucky Queen strike years back and tore up a man and his mule pretty bad and his partner shot at it and it run into the woods. I guess I'll stay here after all.

A grandson of Levon Simmons ~ Southern Oregon

🦍 *The Almeda mine was commonly misspelled "Alameda" at the time; it was even identified incorrectly on many maps. The mine was named "Almeda" after the mine owner's daughter.*

Stamp crushers inside the Almeda Mine

🚶🚶The *Almeda mine is across and down the Rogue River west of Galice, Oregon. In 1922 it still employed close to 250 miners, and even had a floating bridge that spanned the Rogue. That spring, five miners walked off the job and took off downriver in search of their own gold-strike. After two weeks of no discovery, four of them decided to return to Galice, but only one of them made it back to tell the tale of two giant ape-men attacking them and the "giant forest monsters" killing his friends. A search party was dispatched to find the men, but mainly to stop the stories and wild tales in fear that the miners would start quitting their jobs en-masse! It took a week for the searchers to find the attack site, and they only found two of the men. They reported, "The men had been killed by a savage attack on them from some unknown animals of the forest!" The third man was never found, but part of his pants and his hat were there among some "enormous sized" footprints all around the men's bodies! The party returned to the mine with the dead men's packs and the Almeda mine foreman demanded they keep quiet about their grisly discovery, or "lose their jobs." He feared that the workers would all quit out of fear of being attacked! The lone survivor disappeared, and the story was never released until the famous author Zane Grey uncovered the story and wrote about it in an Oregon Trail Magazine article. Zane Grey owned a cabin about 18 miles down the Rogue River from the Almeda, and that's where he wrote his novel, "Rogue*

River Feud."

🚶🚶🚶*The man who wrote this diary may have been referring to J.N. Rainie, who was found dead in his cabin in the late 1920's, and like so many murders that happened along the Rogue River, it was never solved. The Rogue River was known for its disappearances of large numbers of people! Rainie Falls on the Rogue River was named after him.*

Rainie Falls

ALMEDA MURDERS

Publishers note: This is a separate account of the Almeda Mine disaster because there were notations about it in an old miner's journal whose descendants said also worked at the Almeda mine. We have transcribed it exactly as written; with no correction to punctuation, spelling or grammar.

Looking down at the Rogue River from the Almeda Gold Mine

First notation: We lost a party of five off the crew and some of the boys knew they were leavin. They have been planning to go off on their own and have been storing shovels, pans, picks and food back down the river a ways. They have been gathering things each payday and those of us who knew they were planning to go are hoping they hit it rich. And if they do, they're going to have a lot of company.

Second notation: One miner returned today, but the bosses are keeping him away from the rest of us, but word is being spread that they struck out and were working their way back when they was attacked by ape men! Word is that two giant ape men came out of the bushes and tore into the guys, hitting, tearing and beating them. Another party set out to find them, and they had guns, and could not find nobody.

Third notation: Search party came back today with two back packs. I heard that they buried two of the men that were torn up bad, and somebody said their heads were gone! That leaves two that may be floating down the river and the one that lived, he quit but most of us are hearing that the foreman took him to town, gave him his pay, and enough to travel on and kicked him out of town. I heard from one of the shift bosses that the company was trying to keep the story quiet cause they was afraid everybody would quit. The barracks buildings we live in are not that secure and they sit right next to the woods up from the river, so a horse could gallop by and we wouldn't hear it. Also, the road goes just above the buildings and goes right up into the forest. Since this happened we block the door with an iron bar to let us know when it opens. Sure was hoping to strike it rich!

Charley Rindle

BAYOCEAN BIGFOOT

We have spent many enjoyable days hiking at Bayocean☀,
which was at one time, one of the largest cities anywhere on
Oregon's coast. Now it is just a pretty park-like place to hike.

We enjoyed many days taking our dogs with backpacks
carrying food, dogfood and plenty of water. We usually
parked in the designated area on Tillamook Bay and hiked
north following the road past where the bayside hotel and
wharfs had been. We had made this trip about six times, and
were always amazed at the variety of birds that made their
homes here.

A Kansas City real estate developer had built a three story
hotel of concrete, a water system, concrete streets, dance hall,
a huge natatorium, and railroad; and sold over 1600 building
lots, a wharf and a town. Because of an error by the U.S.
Army Corps of Engineers in constructing a single jetty
instead of two, the Pacific Ocean had reclaimed every last
sign that man had ever been here! Mr. Potter was so destitute
over the loss of his dream that one night he walked into the
sea and was never seen again. His creative dream was ruined.

As we normally stopped at certain points for lunch and
breaks, we seldom entered the rather large and overgrown
center part of this isolated peninsula, and where we crossed
near Crab Harbor, this time we took a short trip into the
forested area and followed the deer trails to a broad
depression covered with almost tropical type plants and trees,

and it was welcome shade on a very unusually hot day for the Oregon coast.

Suddenly, a large, brown, shaggy bear-like beast stood up from a small pond, saw us, and made a sort of snort, and tore right up the massive sand dune behind it and disappeared over the top. We just stood there in shock, and even our two dogs didn't seem anxious to go after it. They just looked at us and barked. Neither of us could believe what we had seen, so we went over and looked at the tracks the animal left in the wet sand. One footprint was very clear and it was about twice my size 9 ½'s, and it seemed to have toes much longer than humans.

We climbed up the dune, and the tracks went over the next one and around a large patch of brambles. Judging how fast it had run, we gave up and cut back to the trail that led to the jetties; circled back to the ocean and went south to an ocean side beach trail that would lead us back to the car. As we crossed the beach to the trail two hours later, we saw a footprint that was from the animal, plain as day, right along the wet sand, and it was headed down the beach. There was a narrow spit that it must have gone through to get to the other shore.

That was the place where the peninsula was breached to turn Bayocean into a temporary island years ago when it was destroyed. We stopped at the Tillamook Police Department to tell them what we saw, and just got a knowing smile and a "thanks for the report, but we hear about it each year at least once."

It seems odd that something so strange, and people just seem to accept it, but seldom does it ever get written up, and the explanation we were given is they don't want to scare tourists, as their annual city income is realized over the four month period when they have nice weather each year. We can understand that, being self-employed ourselves.

Frank and Donna S. ~ Portland, Oregon

🦶 *The fascinating story of Bayocean's exciting rise to glory, with people coming from across the United States to purchase home sites, to its tragic death by the sea, as predicted in local Indian tribal legend is a story worth researching. Read "Maimed By The Sea" by authors Bert and Margie Webber. This story will amaze you, as this city, at one time, was one of America's most desired places to own property. The error that caused total and absolute devastation was the construction of a single jetty. Today, the necessary second jetty has joined the first one, but the people and their dreams are all a sad footnote in history.*

Natatorium (background) and dance hall (foreground) at Bayocean, circa 1911-1914

MOUNTAIN APE AT OREGON CAVES

My son bought your book "They Saw Sasquatch," and left it with me to read; he also said you are requesting any stories from other people who have seen these "mountain apes" as us old-timers have always called them. I enjoyed your book, and maybe you can use mine for the next one.

I remember back in 1952 when I saw one. Back then, I lived in Cave Junction, and my parents had a few acres off the main road to the Oregon Caves, which didn't get all that many visitors then. I was a teenager, and I spent a lot of my free time roaming the forests up and around the caves. The rangers knew me and were used to me crawling out of the brush with a squirrel or rabbit in my hand.

I don't know how many people are even aware of it, but there is another cave up there! I came on it by accident when I was climbing along a ledge downhill from the Oregon Caves Chateau. I was armed with my slingshot and a pocket full of rocks, and I could climb like a monkey in those days, and I saw some sort of critter that I thought to be a coyote, but all I saw was a flash out of the corner of my eye, so it could have been a fox; especially that high up the mountain.

I had to go beneath the main road, and I climbed down over a lot of rocks that I think were pushed there when they built the road to the cave. Finally, I ended up on a sort of fairly flat ledge where there was an animal trail that led further down the mountain. Even though it was blocked in places by rocks, I was able to follow it, and all of a sudden, I saw this large shape through the pines up ahead. I thought it was a bear, and I was just about ready to climb up to get away from there quick, because bears are really scary when they've got cubs, when the thing stood up on hind legs and was just staring at me!

I didn't know what to do; I was frozen in place! My feet wouldn't move, and I was just standing there paralyzed, when it kind of snorted and let out a growl, and it turned and ran the other way. That gave me courage, so I cautiously followed it for probably 100 feet further down the slope until I came around a large boulder by a tall pine tree; and there was a cave! I knew I was not following a bear, and whatever it was, had run in fear of me which made me braver than I should have been.

The entrance was back under a ledge, and it was a small opening, which made me duck slightly, which I carefully did. Having no flashlight, I went in just a couple of feet where the cave got bigger, and when my eyes adjusted, I just knelt there and looked around. The cave seemed like it went way back and I could see some reflection that looked like there might be some light from a crack in the ceiling, but that's as far as my young courage went. I carefully backed out the way I came, because even if that mountain ape was scared of me, it was also twice as big as my youthful frame!

So I backed out and just about then, I started shaking all over, and I climbed as fast as I could once my legs started working again. When I got to the road, I made my way up to the main entrance to the monument, where I saw a ranger truck and flagged him down. The man didn't seem surprised about the ape creature, as he said several of the park employees had reported seeing it. Then I told him about the cave, and he knew about it too! He said they believe it was a cavern that stretched east for many miles, but they didn't have funds for exploring it.

When I told my folks about my sighting, I realized my mistake immediately; that mountain was suddenly off limits to me! Not long after that we moved, and I had almost forgot about it until my son mentioned reading your book, so here is my story if you can use it. I wonder if they ever opened that other cave.🦶

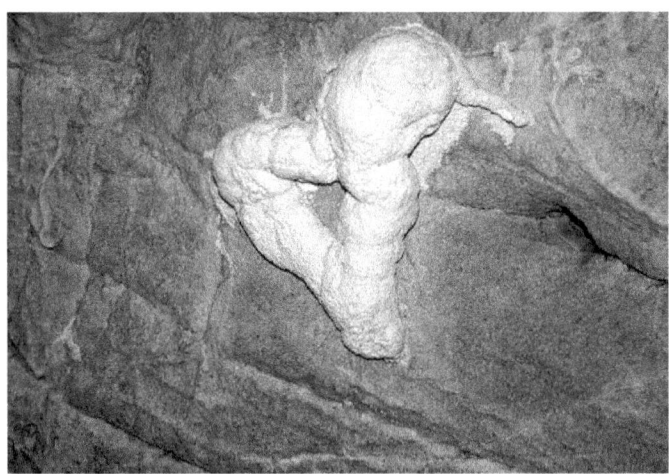

"The Heart" of Oregon Caves

I am also enclosing a brochure that I picked up at The Caves back in the 50s. I recently moved from Prescott to Mesa and came across it as I was packing.

J. McDermott ~ Mesa, Arizona

🏃*It has been recently reported that funding for exploring the additional caves has been authorized. I wish we could have known about this when we were living in that part of the country! The cave is purported to be over 20 miles long, and it is believed that bats have traveled through the cave system between Oregon Caves and Marble Mountain caves outside of Grants Pass.*

WOOKIEES IN THE FOREST

I sometimes contract to do cleanup with the BLM and others outfits that maintain the various camping sites along the Rogue River. After a long winter, a few years back, I was going with a team to prepare the Whisky Creek Cabin🦶 for the new season. We went down to the cabin by 4x4 truck from above on a BLM access road. We relocked the gate when we came through, and as we took the steep, winding road downhill, we could tell the winter had been rough on it and I had to jump out and clear some dead snags from where they had fallen from the slopes above and onto the road. I'd taken the branches and thrown them down the slope below the road.

Whisky Creek Cabin

In one spot, I was out a ways in front of the truck rather than jumping in and out of the cab every few feet, and I hefted a rather large rock that had fallen from the bank above; I rolled it down the slope, and as I watched it careen off a stump, a large bear jumped to the side. Or at least something I thought was a bear; so I walked a few feet further down and right behind the small black bear, followed a large, brown shaggy animal that I thought was a mama bear walking on its hind feet, but it didn't have a snout. It had an ape-like nose, but short ears like a bear, but flatter to its head; and then it came into a clear spot, and both the black bear and I saw it clearly. The bear ran like crazy, and I stood there just staring at the critter. Then it turned off to its left, and in about four leaps, covered over a hundred feet of ground, and it was gone! All of that movement and neither the ape nor the little bear had made a sound.

When I got back in the truck, my super wouldn't believe me. He said maybe the bear, but not the "wookiee," as that was how I described it! So I made him shut off the truck at the next bend and go with me to the stump below, and he did see where something had run, but there were no clear tracks, as the ground was covered with pine needles; but I know what I saw, and when we got back to the shop, I told some of the other guys, and two of the crew and one of the state boys said they had seen these wookiees a couple of times over the years, so I know it was real!

Even the head honcho said he'd heard of people seeing the Bigfoot creatures, and everybody said they moved without sound, even through the trees; like ghosts. I finally gave up telling people, because nobody seems to want to believe, and even those of us who know it is real, eventually give up trying to explain it. I swear to you what I saw was not a bear, and it walked on two legs and had long arms and must have been seven or eight feet tall with shaggy, brown fur and large hands and eyes.

Keith Ryan ~ Brookings, Oregon

🦶*The Whisky Creek Cabin is on the National Historic Register, and the first cabin was built by an unknown miner in about 1880. The spelling of "Whisky" is questionable, as this spelling is for "Scotch," while the miners all drank bourbon whiskey; so it was likely a spelling error. In 1918, Mr. Cy Whiteneck purchased the claim and greatly improved the cabin, built sheds and mined here for 30 years. In 1948, Mr. and Mrs. L.M. Nichols purchased the claim, and in 1957 they hired Mr. Lou Martin to care for their claim.*

Lou greatly improved the property, and even built a solar heated shower and an insulated pantry. You can still see the flume (ditch) which is above the cabin, and carried water to the gully nearby. The flume was used for drinking water, and for hydraulic mining around the cabin and all the way down to the bar where it hits the Rogue River. Mr. Martin even constructed a cable system to easily transport cut logs to his woodshed from nearly 500 feet across the creek so he could keep a constant supply of firewood.

BIGFOOT AT ZANE GREY'S CABIN

I had always wanted to see Zane Grey's cabin since I moved to Grants Pass, but there is no road to it and I'm not a rafter, so after eleven years here, I finally got my chance. A friend and I from Grayback Forestry,⚘ where we both work, had a two week layoff, so we packed up his pickup with camping gear and took off to Marial. That's such a long drive, because the road is so rough, but we finally got started on our hike about 9:30 in the morning; the weather was cool as it was early June. We followed the trail, which is pretty easy, and we kept meeting rafters and hikers all going the other direction quickly down the river.

In the past, I've hiked different sections of the Rogue, and I attempted to see if the property owners along the road by Mt. Bolivar would let me cross their land and hike to the river, because it's only a couple of miles downhill, but they refused to let me go on their land. They must be afraid that more people would hear about and try to do the same thing.

I have read a lot of Zane Grey books and he wrote "Rogue River Feud" while he stayed at his cabin for a month, and I thought it would be fun to see how it would have felt to be there for that long, because I'm sure there weren't any rafts, and very few boats way back then. Now it's a steady stream of rafters; they let about one raft every 10 minutes go by, and it was busy even this early in the season.

Zane Grey Cabin on the Rogue River ~ Image by Bureau of Land Management
Oregon and Washington

Well, we got there on the second day, and there sure wasn't much to see. The signs of his landing strip were there; it was between the cabin and the mountain. I could just picture flying in here, as wild as it must have been back in the 1920s, and it would really have been isolated. The old cabin was boarded up, so we made camp on the flat area along what was his airstrip.

Simply being there was a special treat and we put up our small tarp and cut branches to make a lean-to in a sheltered area under two monstrous pines; then relaxed over a simple meal. It gets dark early in this canyon, and we made sure to have enough firewood, by going up a ways on the mountain to gather enough pieces of dead trees to keep a good flame going. We piled the mostly damp wood near the fire to dry it out as we went. We saw a faint light from a fire on the other side of the river, close to the shore, but it had to be at least a mile upriver from us.

My partner was also a fan of Zane Grey, so just being here was a thrill for both of us, as the author must have enjoyed this place. He had written that some of his happiest memories were of the time he spent fishing on the Rogue River at this spot.

Our fire was burning down around nine o'clock, and we were tired and about done in, when we heard a loud splash at the shore. We could barely see over the brush and weeds by the water, but even with our flashlights we did not see anything. We figured it was a fish jumping, about a half hour later there was a loud crash up the hill behind the lean-to, and several huge rocks came bouncing down near us. We shined our lights up the hillside when a large piece of tree branch landed right on our fire! It scattered ashes and coals all over, and we jumped up and yelled towards the hill, thinking it may be another hiker, but no response.

Then we heard what sounded like a growl or almost a bark and a woof sound, and heard sounds like someone running through the sand and rocks by the shore. Then it got all quiet, and we never heard anything more. I know it took me a long time to get to sleep that night, and the next morning we were up at first light, and one of our backpacks was gone. We searched all around, and Charlie spotted it on the sand down near the water. I had been ripped open, the zipper had been broken, and everything dumped out and scattered. Charlie said he was only missing a couple of Baby Ruth candy bars as far as he could tell. The rest of the contents were dumped like somebody had looked through it and tossed it away.

Well, that was enough exploring for us, and we headed back toward Marial. Walking the trail back, a raft came by and they pulled ashore and said they had seen some kind of large brown animal on the mountain above the cabin, but it disappeared in a few seconds after they started to watch it. They both said it was walking on its hind legs and looked like a very hairy bear!

When we finally got to Marial the next day, we told the folks at the lodge what we had experienced; they laughed and said, "Welcome to the club; you met our Bigfoot!" I guess it was a fairly common event; they said about three people a month had some event like we did. Rather than get alarmed, they seemed to enjoy it, and when they said "Our Bigfoot," we knew we were far from being the first discoverers.

Dave N. ~ Grants Pass, Oregon

🏹*Grayback Forestry, Inc. is a contractor for wildfire suppression, forest restoration and fuels management. They have four bases in Oregon and one in Montana, but they provide equipment and personnel throughout the nation.*

THE SASQUATCH ON THE ROGUE

We are submitting this story that was told by my father, whose father in turn, had told him. Dad wrote it down at the time, as he was an aspiring author, but the various notes he compiled were laying in a cardboard box with old photos and letters that we've been going through. The family remembered this story, because Grandpa had told each of his grandchildren the same tale at various times. What makes it seem like a good thing for the book you're writing is that we all remember it about the same as what Dad had written down.

Although this story was written by Dad, it was told to him by our grandfather Walter Neilsen. This event took place on Whisky Creek near the Rogue River in June of 1941.

I am, with pen in hand, for the records, due to highly unusual experiences with an animal that rumor has reported and that I have seen. I give you my story: I packed a large skid-pack for a long trip. I was going to see a friend down the Rogue at Whisky Creek. I started hiking at the Grave Creek junction with the Rogue River. The trail is pretty good this year; snow is mostly gone from the pockets. There were signs of somebody walking the trail; probably days ago. I'm carrying my H&R .410 shotgun in case I get a grouse or duck. I've plenty of hardtack and taters.

Made it to the Sanderson🦍 place, but won't stop as the boys are down on the river, and my knees don't feel like fighting the hill. I'll catch them on the way back.

It was kind of hard going by China Gulch; some pilgrim tried building a foot bridge, but it's not working very well. I took the time to put a line in the water when I found an easy deer trail down to the river and caught a small salmon; it should make a tasty dinner.

China Gulch

I made it to Whisky Creek🦍🦍 in the late afternoon and found my friend Cy working at the creek. He was working on his flume, which brought water down under pressure from up higher on Whisky Creek. He appears to be making money, but like all these miners, he's short on talking about finding gold; which I can understand, so I never ask any questions about his work.

I've known ol' Cy for long enough to earn his trust, and he invited me to stay for a couple of days; which is why I came. I gave Cy two loaves of bread that I had brought from the bakery for him. Fresh bread seems to be a real treat for the miners along the river. That night for dinner, Cy grilled the salmon I had caught earlier, and it was mighty tasty.

Whisky Creek Cabin

Cy has done a lot since I was here last. His cabin is bigger, and he's built some new sheds. He said he's had somebody or something poking around and he's had to put latches on the doors and nail the windows down. Cy keeps his venison, fish and other game in a sort of root cellar, and he said something busted the door latch, but he heard it and whatever it was, ran like crazy when he fired a shot. At first he thought it was Old man Jensen, but he hasn't been around lately and it's been pretty quiet along the river. He said the

Sanderson boys have also had somebody or an animal breaking into their buildings.

The next morning, I told Cy I'd look around while he was working his claim. So I went down the back hill behind the cabin and behind the root cellar. I found some strange tracks along the creek below the cabin and one set of prints looked at first like a bear, but the prints were a lot bigger. There was one really plain footprint that I couldn't quite cover with my straw fishing hat, so that's like two of my foot size! Must be a big animal, don't know if I really want to run up on it, especially if it's a bear!

The tracks were all over the place in the creek bed, almost like the animal had spent a long time moving around below the cabin. I made sure the shotgun was loaded and I had left my pack in the cabin, so I thought I'd work my way around the hill where Cy was working on a water trough at the river. I figured I'd work my way up the hill and cross to where Cy had cut two trees and had two cross braces on them, with planks running along the poles, making it a pretty nice bridge. It was slippery, but I made it across safely.

I walked carefully in the damp woods and I doubt a deer could have been any quieter, and since I wasn't in a hurry, I enjoyed seeing how quietly I could make my way. The pine needles and wet leaves made my passage as silent as a snake. I wound my way around so I was quite a bit above where Cy was working, and I crouched there and looked over the area; this was above where I had seen all the large prints. Just then something changed in my view, and at first I didn't know what it was, but it was like the landscape changed. Without moving anything but my eyes, I kept staring straight ahead and suddenly it hit me; the large brown bush between two pine trees 30 feet in front of me was looking directly at me! It had eyes!

I could only figure that it had been looking downriver as I was and suddenly it must have smelled me or sensed my presence, and turned to face me; we just stayed where we were staring at each other for what seemed like several minutes and then it was gone. Now this was not a thick forest, but by the time I reacted enough to move the 30 or so feet to where it had been, there it was, about a 100 feet ahead, moving rapidly downhill and into the patch of trees and bushes that lined the Whisky Creek as it made its way toward the Rogue River.

I moved to my left to force the creature toward the place Cy was working, figuring it would turn back when it spotted him, but when I rounded the edge of the heavy brush, it was gone again! I yelled to Cy to head it off, be he just raised up from the sluice and looked at me, and hollered "What?" but he couldn't hear me over the creek's noisy rush. When I got down there, I told him then what happened, and we found a couple of tracks where it must have passed within a few feet of Cy. The tracks it left looked like the ones near the cabin, and now we knew it wasn't humans snooping around, so I helped Cy change the locking systems for the cabin and sheds.

I spent another day and a half visiting, and we even walked up the hill on the logging road that led up the mountain, but never again spotted the ape-looking beast. Cy didn't seem bothered by it, and he said many of the old timers had talked about this animal, so this just added to the many stories among the mining community of the "Ape men of the Rogue."

The remains of Cy Whiteneck's flume ditch

On the way home, I stayed overnight with the Sanderson brothers and when I brought up the experience, they described the animal perfectly. They said it never did any damage, but on occasion they would lose fish from their fish trap, and sometimes some vegetables would disappear, but it never was a cause to worry. They just tolerated it like the area deer.

After this experience, I talked with a lot of miners and loggers in my travels, and the only trouble I ever heard about was a couple of miners from upriver that supposedly were torn to pieces by a couple of big apes, but that happened over 20 years ago.

Submitted by Joel Neilsen ~ Roseburg, Oregon

🐾*The Sanderson brothers built a home on the north side of the Rogue River .6 miles from the present day Grave Creek boat landing. The two-story home was built in about 1940, and the brothers enjoyed a prosperous life mining gold on the river banks below the home. They had a generator, running water, and they were known to have made a very comfortable living. The brothers had a car that they kept on an access road and made frequent trips to town; they were known to often entertain guests. The home was dismantled in 1971 and floods have erased the rest.*

Remains of the generator room at the Sanderson homesite

🐾🐾 *See the chapter "Wookiees In The Forest" for historic information about the Whisky Creek Cabin.*

I THOUGHT THEY HIBERNATED

I am sending you this story on the advice of my wife. This happened to me back in 1974. I was employed as a district sales manager for a major auto manufacturer, and I spent a lot of time visiting auto dealers across my northwest five state territory.

I had spent a couple of days with our franchised dealer in Bend, Oregon, and planned to get an early start the next morning; so that I could get to Eugene, Oregon ahead of the forecasted blizzard, I planned on cutting over through McKenzie Pass. Otherwise, I would have to go up and over the better maintained highway over Mt. Hood to Portland and down to Eugene, which would cost me a day. I left the motel early, as it was already snowing hard, and the local radio station was saying that this was a major blizzard and that McKenzie Pass would likely be closing soon.

When I got up a bit in elevation, it was snowing so hard I could barely see a few hundred feet ahead. Suddenly I passed a state police car that was stopped on the side of the road and the officer was getting something out of his trunk. I later realized it must have been a barricade, as a minute later the radio announcer said that the McKenzie Pass road was closed to all traffic. I breathed a sigh of relief that I had made it. What I had made however, were a couple of hours of the worst conditions I had ever driven in and it gave new meaning to "white knuckle" driving!

The snow banks on each side of the road were so high that glancing to the side all I could see was a white blur and I found that the only way I could even guess where the highway went was to stare straight ahead so my peripheral vision would keep me on the road, because the pine covered mountains shone through as just slightly darker than the snow blanketed road.

After the first hour, the snow on the highway was still only up to a few inches; going slowly, I finally began a very slight descent, which never having driven this road before, I assumed that I had crossed the summit, and after another half hour, the visibility improved and I could actually see the trees on the mountainsides.

McKenzie Pass ~ Image by Oregon Department of Transportation

As I came around a large, sweeping right hand curve, I saw three dark shapes about a quarter of a mile ahead, and they appeared to have just crossed the road, and were climbing a tree covered slope on the right. I slowed down so I could see what they were before they reached the forest. I first thought they were bears, because they were too bulky to be elk, and suddenly, the larger two rose up on two legs and the slightly smaller one (they were both huge) picked up the little one, and they made it into the trees in less than a minute! It must have been 100 yards in deep snow. All I could tell was that they reminded me of shaggy bison, because their fur looked very thick, but their bodies looked like gorillas, but with smaller heads.

Finally, after another hour, I came to a road block and the state police were really shocked to see me. I was just glad to get through the pass, and about two minutes later the snow stopped.

Thomas Frank ~ Phoenix, Arizona

ABOUT THE AUTHORS

Gary and Wendy Swanson have recently located to southern Utah, but lived in Grants Pass, Oregon for the last eight years, where they enjoyed hiking throughout the spring, summer and fall months with their dogs. In addition to their love of hiking, they also enjoy history. Southern Oregon is full of history of gold mining, logging and fishing along the wild and scenic Rogue River; so for them, it has been a great place to research history, explore the countryside and hike all at the same time. Their attention gradually was drawn to the many people they met who had sighted and encountered the Sasquatch. Along with their own experiences, they began to collect stories from others.

www.ingramcontent.com/pod-product-compliance
Lightning Source LLC
Chambersburg PA
CBHW072141280526
45788CB00002B/734